SECRETS TO SCHOOL SUCCESS

Guiding Your Child Through A Joyous Learning Experience

Brandi Roth, Ph.D.
Fay Van Der Kar-Levinson, Ph.D.

Association of Ideas Publishing
Beverly Hills, California

SECRETS TO SCHOOL SUCCESS
Guiding Your Child Through a Joyous Learning Experience

by Brandi Roth, Ph.D. and Fay Van Der Kar-Levinson, Ph.D.

First published in the United States of America in 2002
Association of Ideas Publishing
Brandi Roth, Ph.D.
433 North Camden Drive, Suite 1128
Beverly Hills, CA 90210

www.associationofideas.com

Library of Congress Cataloging-In-Publication Data
Roth, Ph.D., Brandi
SECRETS TO SCHOOL SUCCESS, Guiding Your Child Through A Joyous Learning Experience by Brandi Roth, Ph.D. and Fay Van Der Kar-Levinson, Ph.D.
ISBN 0-9647119-1-5
1st Edition, P. cm. Copyright Number Txu 1-034-393 2002

1. Guidance Through the School Years 2. Elementary and Secondary Education 3. Parent Participation Handbook 4. Secrets to School Success

Printed on recyclable paper
First Edition
10 9 8 7 6 5 4 3 2 1

Cover Design: Kathleen Lowry
Book Design: Terrence McWilliams

ACKNOWLEDGMENTS

Our heartfelt gratitude is extended to our families,
our friends, our colleagues and our clients for their
commitment to learning. Very special thanks from Brandi
to her husband Bruce Clemens and her sister
Carol Chandler for their endless support and assistance
during the writing of this book.

In honor of Brandi's parents, Margaret and Bill,
who volunteered for every school event for their daughters.

In honor of Fay's parents, Dolly and Sieg,
who always encouraged their daughter to learn.

CONTENTS

INTRODUCTION

Secrets to School Success offers parents the tools to help their children have a joyous and positive school experience, gain self-respect and achieve academic and social success.

This book teaches parents how to guide their children through the emotional and educational process of being a student, from kindergarten through high school. It is a reference and resource to use and reuse as situations arise. In an effort to remain gender neutral we are alternately using "your child", "she" or "he" to refer to your child.

The authors' experiences as psychologists and educators provide parents with insight into understanding and identifying their children's educational needs. Parental involvement is crucial to a child's successful education. Parents can help their children have a positive school experience from the first days at a new school, through the selection of classes, extracurricular activities, homework and projects.

The authors provide practical information on how to effectively use your powers and responsibilities as a parent. They suggest strategies for understanding different learning styles, using study skills effectively, homework survival ideas and scheduling your child's after-school life.

The author's first book, **Choosing the Right School for Your Child** is a nation-wide guide and workbook for families selecting elementary, middle and secondary schools for their children. **Secrets to School Success** helps parents and children continue to have an effective and joyous school experience.

We hope you enjoy and value the practical wisdom found in this book.

Brandi Roth, Ph.D.
Fay Van Der Kar-Levinson, Ph.D.

CHAPTER 1

LIFE IN A NEW SCHOOL

Chapter Highlights

Life in a new school is an exciting adventure. But whether a child is entering kindergarten or seventh grade, just finding his way around campus on that first day is a major accomplishment. Some children sail in and adapt to the experience of a new school as if it were a continuation of their previous year. Others find the transition a daunting challenge.

In this chapter we will discuss how to prepare your child for life in a new school or a return to school after a holiday or long absence and offer ways to help ease the transition.

PERIOD OF ADJUSTMENT

Each child adapts to life in a new school in his or her own way. The transition for some children is effortless, but many need reassurance; they want to know what will be expected of them and need to be well prepared ahead of time for what they will face. The period of adjustment can last anywhere from a few days to a few weeks.

Here is what Travis, age 11, told incoming middle school students about starting their new school:

> *"When you change to a new school, there are a lot of problems you must solve. The problem I had was I didn't have any friends in my new classes. To fit in, I needed to make new friends by being friendly to everyone. If I hadn't been friendly, I wouldn't have any new friends to do things with.*
>
> *When I went to my new school, there was a new campus and I got lost on it. I looked at the map in the 'Binder Reminder' and found my way around. If I didn't remember my way around, I would be late and get 'trash pick-up.' There were new rules, which I learned by reading them over and over again. If I forgot them and did something bad, I would get in trouble. Changing schools can always bring problems, but most of them can be solved."*

What Travis describes is that sensation of being lost, physically as well as emotionally, and of looking for campus landmarks and friendships to anchor him to the new school. Although he was entering middle school, what he says applies to "first days" at all levels.

KINDERGARTEN THROUGH ELEMENTARY SCHOOL

Ten Things to Do Before the School Year Begins

1. Before the first day, tour the school with your child to help him become familiar with the surroundings. If you are unable to visit inside the buildings, at least drive by, park and walk around the grounds.

2. Find out who the teacher or teachers will be and where your child's classrooms are located. Form a parent-teacher relationship at the beginning. When you meet with the teacher privately, ask how student problems are handled. Alert the teacher to any specific requirements for your child.

3. Meet the school personnel. Make class selections if they are offered. Learn field trip schedules and become a parent volunteer when possible.

4. Learn which clothing styles are appropriate for school and within dress code restrictions, and buy some of these clothes before school starts.

5. Settle the transportation issue. For carpools, ask at school who lives in your neighborhood. For walking or bicycling, plan and practice routes before school starts.

6. Arrange for your child to meet and make play-dates with new classmates, particularly those who live nearby. This will ease the transition into the new setting, make your child comfortable with carpool mates and provide friends who are ready to share homework or play after school.

7. Inquire about school lunch policies, including the amount of time allotted for lunch. Consider the pros and cons of bringing lunch versus buying it at school. Learn what kind of food is offered and how payment is arranged—cash or lunch tickets.

8. Ask if there are backpack requirements or supplies you need to purchase. (See Be Prepared With School Supplies in Chapter 13.)

9. Check out the location of the restrooms.

10. Find out if there is a Wishing Well Room or special area for rest or quiet play.

Visual and Auditory Testing

Not all schools require students to have a physical check-up before school starts, but most require an immunization record. In addition, a visual examination and auditory screening are advisable.

Ideally, visual checkups should include color blindness, visual field, near and far vision, ability to accommodate from near to far and back again, and visual perceptual skills. This test should be repeated yearly or as needed.

Much of children's work in education requires auditory discrimination ability. When problems with this skill go undetected, a child's learning aptitude and behavior may be incorrectly assessed. The auditory screening should determine your child's ability to discriminate and sequence sounds; his hearing may be fine, but he may not be able to detect subtleties *between* sounds such as "b" and "d".

If your child has difficulty listening or following directions, you might consider having an audiologist check his hearing and/or a psychologist check auditory discrimination and auditory processing of information.

Relieving Separation Anxiety on the First Few Days of School

It is not uncommon for children to wake up the first few days of school with complaints of, "I have a stomachache" or screaming hysterically, "I won't go, you can't make me, I'm never going back to school." They may be afraid of the separation from home and parents, especially after a relaxing, wonderful summer.

The new and unfamiliar can be scary. When a child does not know what to expect, anxiety may begin to build. How do you prepare your child for staying at school without you? One charming and wise woman had her granddaughter sit at a desk and scribble in a notebook as practice for what it would look like and feel like to be in kindergarten when it started a few weeks later. Here are some other ideas to consider:

1. Most adults remember their first day of kindergarten. Hearing a parent share his or her first-day-of-school experiences can be enormously helpful if relayed with a sense of humor, support and love.

2. If your school arranges a party for incoming kindergartners before school starts this allows students to see the classroom and meet their teacher and classmates. Older children transferring to a new school may be assigned a "buddy" who will contact them before the year begins.

3. If your school provides a student contact list, you can invite a classmate to your house before school starts and make carpool arrangements. If the school does not provide such a list, ask for names of children who live in your neighborhood or zip code. Occasionally, a school will assign an incoming family a "buddy family" who has a child in the same grade level.

4. If you know your child has a difficult time letting you go, you might ask school administrators whether there is a policy allowing mothers and/or fathers to stay with their children at the beginning of the first day.

5. Put an extra (healthy) snack in his lunch, either to share with a friend or to eat if he gets hungry on the way home; but be careful not to use food as a means of dealing with feelings and emotions.

6. Mementos from family and home provide reassurance. Your child could take along a comfort item on the first day of school. A picture of his dog, mom, dad, sister, brother, the family, the grandparents, a postcard of some special place, a lucky rock or other small item to keep in his pocket for comfort are all appropriate. It is particularly comforting to discover a loving letter or note from dad or mom in a lunch bag or even a note from the family pet.

> *Allison, age five, asked her mom for a piece of paper with a lipstick kiss, a drop of her perfume and a love note on it. She carried it and a family photo with her every day during her first week at school.*

7. A small board game such as chess, checkers or a travel word game could be brought for recess and lunchtime. This gives a young student an activity to look forward to. (Make sure this meets school rules.)

8. Send small change along with your youngster for buying snacks or using a pay phone. If necessary to call home regularly, consider teaching an older child to use a prepaid phone card.

What If Your Child Experiences Severe Separation Anxiety?

A nurturing teacher, who is sensitive to these kinds of issues, can help fearful children quickly adjust to school. In addition, both parents and children need to understand that separation anxiety is neither a flaw nor an indication that these children will be clingy, shallow, or dependent adults. In fact, they are likely to be loyal and supportive in friendships and relationships as the years go by.

Separation anxiety can be an aspect of a common developmental stage and often indicates that a child forms intimate, strong emotional bonds. Rather than saying, "Amy is so dependent, she won't let me go," think of Amy as someone who forms deep attachments and strong bonds, but who takes her time to form *new* attachments.

To ease the anxiety, parents can use some or all of the following strategies:

♦ Parents need to ask their children open-ended questions that promote information gathering. Investigate what is going well and what is not, and identify their greatest fears.

♦ Ask the younger child: "What made you smile today? Did you hear a story today? Did you paint a picture?" These might produce "yes or no" answers. Take the opportunity to explore and have your child say what was it about a picture or a story he liked.

♦ Ask your child what would help him feel safe and comfortable. If the child says, "I need you to stay all day long," calmly explain, "That's not possible, but I can stay for fifteen minutes."

♦ You can reduce your child's anxiety by working a few hours at the school, perhaps in the library or the office, if this is workable.

♦ You could walk your child to his classroom or go to breakfast together before school. You might move your car or run an errand and come back quickly to reassure your child.

◆ Some parents, who have young children with severe separation anxiety, benefit from giving a pager or cell phone number to the teacher. The child does not need to know about the pager; however, its use can lessen a parent's fear of being unavailable if a child has a severe anxiety episode.

◆ For an older student, make sure he has a watch and promise to be out in front on the sidewalk (or a special meeting place) at a specific time, e.g. 2:45 p.m. This will give him a clear picture of when and where he will see you again.

◆ Assure your child that you will be fine so he will not worry about you.

◆ Arrange a separation plan with your child prior to the first day of school. To avoid disappointments, be sure to check with administrators ahead of time to ascertain whether your plan is in compliance with school policy.

> For example, before Daniel's first day at kindergarten, his parents asked him to tell about his concerns and what would make him feel comfortable. His mother told him she would stay until he felt comfortable enough for her to leave, and they agreed on a signal that Daniel would give her when he was ready. However, school policy did not permit parents to stay with their children and Daniel's mother could not stay in class. Not surprisingly, Daniel was disappointed. He said, "You promised me you wouldn't leave until I was okay and then you left me before I signaled!"

◆ If your child has a hard time letting you go, see if his school offers organized activities in the morning, so he can play with other children before the official day begins. The keys to a successful separation are structure and organized activities.

◆ Be aware that your body language communicates your feelings to your child. You may unwittingly encourage your child to be uncomfortable. For instance, if you hesitate, your child may pick up your uncertainty. It is helpful to create a routine way to say good-bye.

◆ In cases where it is harder for your child to separate from one parent but not the other, if possible, trade off taking your child to school.

◆ It is difficult to leave while your child is crying, even when you know your child will adapt after just a few minutes. Arrange to be called if your child does not stop crying within thirty minutes, because no child should cry continuously for longer than that. Then meet with your child's teacher to agree upon ways to cope with your child's separation anxiety. To reassure yourself and your child, have a planned activity to which your child can look forward, and tell him, "The teacher has my number in case of emergency." Additionally, it helps to say, "Be sure to remember things you do today so you can tell me about them when I pick you up."

•   Some children cope with separation anxiety by creating a list or agenda for the day. They want an orderly plan instead of moment-by-moment events. Prepare a handmade or commercial calendar and update it daily, or at least once a week, by putting each day's plan on it. Apply stickers indicating the weather forecast so your child will know to take a jacket. For a child who is a bit on edge about going to school in the morning, it can be comforting to know there are definite activities planned after school. The calendar will also be useful when parents leave on a trip. Placing a sticker of a plane or car on the dates of departure and return will help quantify the time and the number of nights you will be away, and your child can plan his activities accordingly.

•   Transitions from the school back to the home at the end of the day can also create difficulties for children, especially if the person who picks the child up is not a parent. Brandi suggested planning a "surprise". One grandmother we know tried this approach with her reluctant grandson:

> "Someday, I hope you'll surprise me when I arrive, by jumping up, telling your teacher good-bye, and saying 'Hi!' to me, so we can start our afternoon together."

The very next day, her grandson did exactly what she asked, and he has continued to leave class with her quite calmly ever since.

If you know your child has severe separation problems, be sure to ask the school about their policies. Although not common, certain schools will ask children with persistent separation anxiety to leave the school. In cases where severe anxiety persists beyond three weeks, you might want to consult with a specialist.

Dealing With Your Own Separation Anxiety

Here is a list of things parents say that are guaranteed to *increase* separation anxiety:

- "I felt lost without you."
- "I kept walking by your room."
- "The dog cried all day."
- "Your little brother/sister missed you all day."

Statements like these not only will magnify separation anxiety in your child but also will create guilty feelings for having a good time at school and not missing you.

Parents may also find the separation difficult. Your child may have been with you every day but now is growing up and will be gone for several hours each day. Identify what you will miss and make your own plan. Many parents have found it helpful to spend time with other parents of kindergartners.

Some of the methods that we have used to help children and parents with separation anxiety are:

- Arrange how you will say good-bye each morning. Your ritual could be to walk your son to the classroom door, say good-bye, have a quick kiss and a hug or say good-bye at the gate and wave when he gets to the door.

- You and your child could select a special object such as a rock that he will touch during the day and know that you are thinking about him. If your child's clothing lacks pockets, one idea is to sew on a secret pocket to hold a love note, toy, photo or reminder of the parent.

- Arrange a task for your child to do as soon as he arrives at school. This will take teacher cooperation too. Some examples are cleaning the chalkboard, watering the plants, lining up the chairs, or taking care of classroom pets.

List some of your ideas here:

_____

_____

_____

Reunions

Many children like to be greeted with information about after-school plans. When a parent explains what the plan is for the afternoon and then asks the child to discuss his feelings about the plans, the child feels like he is part of the process. Review the schedule and provide enough details about who will pick up your child and whose mom or dad will be there. This gives your child an opportunity to speak his viewpoint, as well as be prepared for what will be happening.

Children enjoy telling about their day on their own terms. Try to reunite with welcoming greetings such as, "Hi. I'm happy to see you. Let's plan our afternoon activities together." Show interest in your child's day and express happiness to see him again. Start gently, saying, "It's good to see you. I'm curious to hear about your day." Avoid saying "I missed you" because it induces guilt instead of the freedom to have a good time apart from the family.

When you leave your child at school, you may wonder what is happening. How do you get that information? The temptation is to quiz the child, asking questions like, "Did you make new friends? Did you sit next to anyone you like especially?" One of the main complaints we often hear children express is, "They quiz me about everything."

"How was your day?" is a welcome greeting to some children, but frequently they complain that they feel pressured to answer on the spot. Some children need to think about experiences before they talk about them and like to let thoughts about the day percolate; they may save their stories for dinner or even bedtime, which is another good reason for bedtime rituals and quiet time. Saying, "I would enjoy hearing about your day sometime tonight" could feel inviting.

Transition Times

There are many transition times for children during their school years. These transitions include entering preschool, kindergarten, middle school or high school, and transferring to a new school. Returning from a long absence, a summer break or a holiday break can also be challenging for some children.

Eight-year-old Martin neglected to mention to his parents that he was having a hard time adjusting to being back at school. Two weeks passed before the teacher phoned to say Martin was disruptive and having a difficult time since returning to class. She called it uncharacteristic of him. When asked about the situation, Martin said, "I don't know, I'm just having a hard time."

Because Martin had not told his parents that he felt a build-up of pressure and that he was struggling and feeling anxious, the situation grew bigger and more significant than it would have, had it been addressed earlier. Please invite your child to tell you if he is having a problem as soon as he knows. This will relieve the pressure and avoid setting off a big explosion. When this child told us, "I can feel pressure building up when a lot of things are going bad," we gave him opportunities to notice how that felt in his body. That way he could tell us problems were mounting up as soon as he recognized the signs. To feel balanced he can express his feelings and describe behaviors he plans to act on or ways to think about the needs.

When a child is regularly misbehaving, we suggest that the parent visit the school and either sit in the back of the classroom or tutor another child who may need help. The presence of a parent in the place where the child is having difficulty can often modify that behavior. In one case, a child so disliked having his parent in class he immediately changed his behavior. In another case, a girl who was struggling with transition was so happy when her mother was present that we reversed the situation. The mother's visit was used as a reward for attendance, participation and completing her work.

When a young child is adjusting to a new school or making a transition, negative behaviors may also appear or increase at home. Tantrums, wanting more snacks or needing excessive attention from mom or dad can occur at the start of kindergarten.

At times of transition, a parent may need to take a personal day off from work. Companies usually permit employees to take at least three personal days per year, so if your child needs you, we urge you to take advantage of this option.

Use some of the strategies mentioned earlier in the chapter to make transitions back to school as well as to a new school successful.

Beware of Creating "Participatory Anxiety"

Overestimating possible problems can result from parental comments such as: "You may feel uncomfortable. We'll help you with any problems." A discussion is appropriate but too many repetitions may be harmful. Encourage and support your child with balanced statements such as, "Starting a new school can be exciting and scary."

This also applies to over-selling the new school by repeating statements such as, "You're so lucky. You get to go to this school!" Like seasoning a fine meal, there can be too much of a good thing.

Parents might inadvertently transfer their concerns to their child. Frequently intruding in other aspects of a child's life can rob the child of his own inner process about an experience. Too many questions, such as, "Luke, do you like that? What do you think of that?" can cause a child to grow up with feelings, thoughts and ideas produced on command, instead of spontaneously. Do occasionally ask how things are going, or create an atmosphere that says you are always ready to listen.

What To Do When Your Child is Unhappy at the New School

What if your child says, "I hate school and I never want to go back"? Parents feel tempted to try to fix it—or crusade to change it—or blame the child. "I did all this for you, jumped through hoops, and you aren't even trying."

Often it is the parent, not the child, who is unhappy. Parents who were happily involved at nursery school occasionally experience difficulty in adapting to a longer day without their child and to less direct involvement at the new school.

Sometimes the new school may fit everyone in the family except the crucial member—the student. We have seen cases where parents were more enthusiastic than their child. Jessica told us, "Daddy is so excited about my new school. If I could only put him in my uniform and send him to school."

We have also seen cases where expectations were so high that even though the adaptation was going well, the child perceived it differently. After the first week of seventh grade one girl told us, "I thought I would have five best friends, but I've only met two girls I like."

This is a good time to talk with your child about friendships. If you feel your child is not integrating well after school starts, ask your child and ask the teacher for the names of two or three classmates your child might get along with, and schedule play dates for her.

Knowing When to Change Schools

If your child seems truly unhappy, first ask yourself whether your child usually needs a great deal of time and support during transitions. If so, be patient. Write a thorough list of pros and cons of the school; and because some items will be more significant, weight the list accordingly. Ask yourself the global questions: What are your long-range goals versus your immediate goals?

Evaluate the following factors when trying to decide whether you are going through the throes of adjustment or really need to move to a new school:

♦ Is your child unhappy every morning on the way to school?

♦ Does the administration support your concerns or your desires for your child? Do they listen to you?

♦ Does the philosophy of the school, in practice, live up to the reasons that you chose this school?

Make a change when the school curriculum no longer matches your child's needs and abilities, or when your child is no longer flourishing in the environment. Make a change when you realize you are not comfortable with the philosophy of the school. Another reason for change, one that is extremely sensitive, occurs when your child has been labeled unjustly or in a manner that will never be productive.

If you have serious doubts, start looking at other schools. Do not wait too long for things to get better. Sometimes they do not.

What to Do If You Change Your Mind

If you decide to change schools, quietly begin to explore your alternatives. Find out about registration policies for your local public school or how to acquire a transfer permit to a school of your choice. Or, if you have identified a few private schools that you think will be a better match for your child, start the application process.

Some schools are threatened by your application to other schools, so wait to ask for teacher evaluations until you are far enough along in the process to be fully committed to a change. It is awkward to give a teacher an evaluation form, which is a clear indication your child is considering a school transfer. It is best for your child and his teacher to focus on the learning process for as long as possible.

How to Consistently Evaluate the School Year

Talk with your child about how the year is progressing. We suggest that parents schedule a quarterly meeting with their child. It can be held either informally, such as on the way home from school, or at a more formal time and place, for example, Sunday after dinner. As you evaluate each quarter, you can get a sense of change. Was there a difficult transition at the beginning that has improved? Is your child learning and enthusiastic about his studies?

With a younger child, you may ask, "What is the best thing that your teacher does during the day?" "What did you least like about your day?" "What are the best features?" "What features does he like least?" "What is most helpful to him as a student?"

If your child comes home from school grumbling about homework, but excited about the science project, that may be a typical student reaction. However, if you have concerns about your child's progress at school, it is crucial that you make an appointment with his teacher or an administrator and express your concerns. This is your best opportunity to determine if this is the right school for your child.

You may be delightfully surprised at how supportive the administrators and teachers are to your predicament. Evaluate how they respond to your sense that this may not be the right school for your child. Do they come up with a series of positive strategies? If your child has not made friends, will they generate a list of children for possible play dates? Do they encourage a buddy system at lunch to try to integrate your child into the school's social structure? Do they find a buddy parent for you so that you can learn more about the school? Do they agree to give you periodic feedback? Or, do they agree that your child would fit better at another school and if so, will they help you find another school? If administrators and/or teachers take a negative or dogmatic position or do not support you, this is a good indication that this school is the wrong place for your child.

Retention

Whether or not to retain a child or to repeat the same grade at school is a frequently asked question. Sometimes the answer is obvious, and parents and teachers, schools administrators and the child agree. Often the decision is not obvious. When a child transfers to a new school, the parents and the school must decide whether to accelerate the child to a higher grade or to retain her at the current grade level. The age range of students in any particular classroom can vary from one to two years. As a general rule, we believe it is best to retain a child early in her school career. By puberty we notice that children who are older than their classmates tend to be some what stronger emotionally and academically.

Gather information before you make this decision:

- Conference with your child's teacher and other involved professionals
- Review work samples
- Administer formal assessments
- Review all academic records
- Consider psychological needs
- Discuss social emotional levels
- Obtain a medical evaluation
- Review standardized school tests
- Review report cards and teacher comments

There are many factors to consider in making this decision. They include:

- Maturity
- Self esteem
- Birth date
- Friends and social skills

- Family factors: birth order and grade level of siblings
- Speech and language skills
- Attitude of the child toward retention
- Special learning needs
- Medical concerns
- Psychological needs
- School requirements for promotion

For a detailed discussion of school choice and retention please refer to our book **Choosing the Right School for Your Child**.

Understanding Teachers

Caring teachers and making new friends are crucial to adjusting to a new school or new grade. Children frequently discuss teachers in terms of being nice or mean. Some students, particularly in the early years, are sensitive to the perception of their teacher as someone who likes them. When these children perceive a teacher as being mean, they often pull back in their studies, refusing to work for someone they do not like.

During a child's school career, there are likely to be wonderful teachers. There may be others who are too strict, too permissive, have personality problems or seem cold or distant. A strict teacher may want things only one way, her way, and may not be willing to look at other viewpoints. Talk to your child about the qualities that make an outstanding teacher. Desirable qualities to look for include:

- Cares about and connects with children
- Has a love of children
- Listens actively to children
- Has an enthusiasm for teaching
- Has strong teaching skills and knows the subject matter
- Is interested in the needs of the students
- Recognizes learning abilities, learning differences and the uniqueness of each child
- Is patient
- Manages a classroom well, keeps order with fairness
- Knows the children

- Keeps the students informed of daily work
- Regularly notifies students of their progress
- Welcomes parent involvement in the classroom
- Is open to new ideas and suggestions
- Is flexible
- Relates well to other teachers
- Is respected by the faculty

Heather, age eleven, explains the qualities of a good teacher: "I think that teachers should be relaxed and not be so strict that children are scared of them, because if they are scared they won't like the teacher and they won't enjoy the class. If the teacher is boring, you might fall asleep in the class and then you won't learn. When a teacher is boring, you just look forward to the end of the class instead of learning the subject."

Strategies for Relating to a Teacher

You can teach your child to understand that people behave in ways that look mean but are not truly rooted in meanness. This just may be the way the teacher disciplines, or maybe the teacher is having problems at home. Teach your child some empathetic responses as well as some humorous ways to cope. Some parents have the child prepare an "awful list." After school ask your child, "What were the five or ten worst things?" or "Did you catch her being good?" "What are some caring ways you noticed?"

Amy, age seven, found that her mother listened attentively every day after school as she catalogued a list of complaints about her teacher at her new school. Amy said she had no friends and the teacher never called on her. Her mother went to school trying to "fix" all the horrible problems. Luckily, the school administrator had recently visited this classroom and saw Amy actively engaged with other children and called on by the teacher. They arranged for a third person to observe, and he confirmed the administrator's conclusions. Amy needed a meeting with the teacher and reassurance about what steps were being taken to notice and respond to her.

If your child is placed in a class where there are many discipline problems, quality teaching becomes much more difficult. When there are very few discipline problems, the teacher is able to be more relaxed and maintain a permissive environment. The students also feel more relaxed and find it easier to get work done without distractions.

There are, however, occasions when a teacher just may not be an ideal match for your child. This is the time to take action.

Michael, age ten, had a sarcastic fifth grade teacher who thought she was being funny. Her style was highly offensive to Michael—so much so that he had stomachaches before going to class. One day he begged his mother to let him stay home. When the teacher called roll and got to his name she said, "Oh good, Michael isn't here." (Michael heard about this from another child.) That episode indicated that Michael's feelings were justified. His mother brought the matter to the attention of the principal and as a result, Michael was transferred to another class and the teacher was counseled by the administration.

Become Actively Involved at Your Child's School

One way to become involved is to volunteer as a room parent in elementary school, or as a class representative at the middle or high school level. If you have enjoyed that involvement, you can do more in the second year. If you wish greater active involvement on the parent board (Parent Teacher Association-PTA, Parent Teacher Student Association-PTSA, Parent Faculty Organization-PFO, Parent Teacher Organization-PTO), volunteer to become recording secretary. By choosing that position, you are likely to learn the complete political workings of your school. Other entry-level positions include fundraising or hosting teacher appreciation events. For your third year, you could run for parent board president or executive vice-president. Usually there is a progression, ladder or pattern for school leadership positions.

As part of your parent involvement, ask the school to give you as much advance notice as possible for any school day student activity, such as a school play or other production your child will participate in. This will increase your chance of scheduling time to be available.

MIDDLE SCHOOL AND HIGH SCHOOL TRANSITIONS

For the older child, entering middle school and high school may be fraught with more complications. Teenagers approach the transition with a more complex set of needs and expectations, including the need to feel secure about the following issues:

- Their school work is manageable and appropriate
- They will develop friendships
- They will be able to handle sports
- They will be able to navigate the route across campus and get to class on time
- They can handle a locker and have time to go from locker to class
- If there are no lockers, being able to carry and organize numerous books and supplies around the campus (backpacks on wheels)
- They have time to go to the restroom
- They are safe in restrooms

Small reassurances help students who are new to middle and high school understand that these challenges are normal and manageable. Ask your teen how the transition is progressing.

Communicating About School with Your Teenager

Communication is a delicate balance. You may have to let your youngster settle in before inquiring about his day. Avoid hitting him with a barrage of questions when you first see him after school. If your teenager feels you are prying, he will often shut down and act sullen. Observe his body language when you ask questions, and pace yourself accordingly.

The car is a good place for conversation, but wait to see if your child is ready to talk. Students need to decompress from the day before they volunteer information. When you greet your child, your eagerness to discover what happened in his day may be perceived as a formal inquisition. Instead of starting with, "How was your day, what happened?" try a reentry comment or a welcome such as, "It's good to see you" or "Do you want to plan something for this afternoon or evening?" If that goes well, then you might ask, "Tell me what they're talking about in history?" Or "Who is in your home room?"

Make a point of remembering details from these conversations and build up a base of information to demonstrate that you are listening to your child and that you are interested. Remember his friends' names. Your child will know that you have really tuned in when you incorporate this information into your conversation. For instance, when you ask about a new friend say, "Did you have a chance to talk to Angie about the coincidence that both of you come from Colorado?" Sometimes a general conversation about unrelated topics can lead into a discussion about an area of concern.

Helping the Older Child to Progress Through the School Year

We suggest that you make it a point to regularly ask your older child if he needs help with schoolwork. The aid of a tutor might be appropriate.

Know when to expect grade cards and the schedule for mid-term and final exams. Ask your teen if he is prepared for tests and allow ample time to provide help if he is not ready. Follow up after exams by asking, "What was most helpful for you in your studying? Were you able to demonstrate your knowledge on the test?"

Pay attention to your child's workload. Students recognize when assignments are meaningful. Piling on extra work seems like punishment to them.

Jessica, age fourteen, cried in frustration every day because she was not sufficiently challenged at school. Unfortunately, her school's response to her pleas for more challenging material was to put her in the library away from her classmates and give her extra work. In essence, she felt punished, rather than rewarded, for her intelligence, and misunderstood for her learning differences.

Planning an exciting or creative project with a youngster like Jessica is more likely to interest her. In addition it would help her feel a part of the decision.

Watch your child for signs of trouble. Abnormal behavior in an older child may be an indication of problems at school.

Justin, age fifteen, became belligerent toward the family after starting high school. He teased his sisters as a way of acting out. This was a warning to the parents that they needed to find out what was going on, rather than punish him.

When his family sought therapy for him, it was revealed that his high school was more difficult than his middle school. He was no longer the straight "A" student, although, even with the transition and the difficulty of the school, he was doing very well in all subjects except math.

We agreed that Justin would meet with the Dean alone. When he explained his problems with math, the Dean told him she had been an algebra teacher, and she offered to tutor him. They devised a plan to meet secretly and then surprise the teacher with his progress.

When Justin told his parents of the plan, they were ecstatic. The antagonistic behavior and acting out at home discontinued.

Lunch Periods

The decision to bring lunch or to buy lunch can be complicated for a student. Sometimes you may discover that what appears to be a school phobia is actually a lunch period or cafeteria phobia. A teenager thinks "How do I get through that horrendous lunch period where it seems as if there are three thousand people in the cafeteria?" "Where do I get my lunch?" "How do I find a place to sit?" "Will people let me sit with them?" "How do I handle rejection when I ask to sit with someone and they say they are saving this seat for Francine?" Attempting to minimize these fears can exacerbate a child's silent fretting.

To alleviate these worries, suggest that your child call another student in the evening and arrange to meet and go to the cafeteria together the next day. Your child could identify a friend or acquaintance in the class period before lunch to walk with and say, "Let's have lunch together" or "Can I join you?"

Recommend that your child select a special part of the cafeteria as his area and carve that large area into smaller spaces. Tell your teen that if he cannot find someone to sit with, he might take something to read or look at or some schoolwork to accomplish; someone may join him. If the school allows it, bring a miniature deck of cards and play Solitaire. This activity may also pull other kids to him.

Some schools offer a choice of hot or cold lunches and special lunches may be available on certain days of the week. If there is a choice of a regular cafeteria, fast food or food from a catering truck, you may need to supervise your child's choices and/or set a financial limit. One mother was spending $15 per day because her son was buying expensive food from the catering trucks parked outside his school.

Federal funding and lunch-assistance programs may mean long cafeteria lines. Enterprising teachers and principals give front-of-the-line passes as incentives for parent participation, discipline, cooperation or high achievement.

If conflict arises because your child wants to buy lunch at school and you want to pack his lunch, suggest a compromise: buy lunch at school on certain days and take lunch on others. Some children are socializers at lunch. Some children race through lunch or throw half of it away to get out to play or to get the best ball court. Some children trade food at lunch. Have an agreement about what trading is acceptable to you.

If you have a fussy eater, take him to the market and make a list of what appeals to him. Post the list at home and plan lunches around it.

ACTIVITIES
TO HELP YOUR CHILD ADJUST TO SCHOOL

Ask your child's opinion about the qualities of an outstanding teacher and list them here.

_____

_____

_____

_____

_____

Ask yourself which teacher is the one that you think you will remember as being the most wonderful teacher your child had at school and say why. Have your child do the same.

_____

_____

_____

_____

_____

Parents can be involved by listing qualities of the teacher they remember from their own childhood as being the most wonderful and relate facts that they remember after all these years.

_____

_____

_____

_____

_____

Plan a new strategy for adjusting to school.

_____

_____

_____

_____

_____

Things that helped me my first day:

_____

_____

_____

_____

_____

CHAPTER 2

EMPOWERMENT

Chapter Highlights

EMPOWERMENT STRATEGIES FOR PARENTS
  Optimism
  Parenting Styles

CHILDREN HAVE FEARS
  Anxious Feelings
  Daily Strategies to Lessen Fears
  Worry vs. Wonder
  Anticipatory Anxiety

EMPOWERMENT STRATEGIES FOR CHILDREN
  Advice to Help Your Child In and Out of the Classroom
  Actions Children Can Take to Increase Empowerment
  Winners and Losers
  Motivation
  Encouraging Creativity and Productivity

EMPOWERMENT ACTIVITIES

Teachers and parents influence children. They can scare them or flood them with information or they can educate them in a way that increases their knowledge and empowers them to take action to solve problems.

In this chapter, we will show you how to teach your child to cope with problems and fears. The most effective way to empower your child is by giving them strategies for dealing with challenges. Children may not automatically know how to reduce their anxiety. However, children who learn to look for solutions and take action in the face of fear do not feel helpless or defeated. They feel competent and become action-oriented problem-solvers who make the world a better place. Then, as they get older, your child will know what to do when fear wells up. This ability is called empowerment.

EMPOWERMENT STRATEGIES FOR PARENTS

School success requires parent involvement, well-defined school curriculums, fair-minded teachers and children who have tools to feel competent. Many experts have promoted empowerment of parents, teachers and children for decades. William Glasser, M.D. who originally authored *Reality Therapy* which evolved into *Choice Theory* has excellent ideas about empowerment and education. His quality school and choice theory ideas are being implemented worldwide. Quality schools are described in the following way:

- A warm, supportive classroom environment
- Students performing useful work
- Students asked to do the best they can
- Students asked to evaluate their own work and improve it
- Students achieve satisfaction about their work
- Success achieved through quality work
- Strong relationships connecting teachers, students, and parents leading toward school success

We hope that a commitment to quality schools will become commonplace in our lifetime. Children who have confidence in their ability to learn make better commitments to studying and participating in the school process. Improving school quality requires everyone's commitment to creating safe schools in which children feel competent and empowered and in which they enjoy learning.

Optimism

Along with heirlooms, families hand down traditions of how they view the world to subsequent generations. Some families see life in a negative light, where everything is viewed through a filter of, "can't," "watch out," "don't," fatalism, pessimism, hopelessness and worry. This approach sometimes appears under the guise of, "I am protecting you for your own good."

Optimistic families hold the belief that happiness is possible. Their children see life as an unfolding adventure, and they stay open to new experiences. They feel hopeful and learn to take the good with the bad and make the best of any situation.

One family had two grandmothers, both of whom lived into their nineties. One grandmother had economic privilege and opportunity; yet, she consumed her life with worry, thereby limiting her potential and her experiences. The other grandmother had fewer economic opportunities and greater hardship. Because she remained curious, open-minded and optimistic throughout her life, she empowered herself, expanded her opportunities, and increased the enjoyment of everyone around her.

Parenting Styles

The first step in empowering your child is to become aware of your parenting style. Effective parents talk about a situation in terms of past, present and future. They ask questions, such as what happened, how do you feel about it now, what is the future plan for solving it?

Many decades ago, a research study examined differences in parenting styles. The four identified were:

1. Authoritative warm
2. Authoritative cold
3. Permissive warm
4. Permissive cold

The study revealed that children who develop the highest self-esteem, the greatest sense of confidence, the highest functioning level and the most independence are more likely to have been parented in an authoritative warm manner. Their parents set clear limits for them but they solicit their children's input and take it into consideration before making final decisions.

Children raised in a permissive warm home also fare quite well. This style is characterized by parents who hold discussions with their children but who may cave in to their demands a bit too readily.

Parents who take an authoritative cold approach, which allows or provides no discussion of options, are more likely to have youngsters with delinquency problems. These children are often left with no outlet except anger, and in reaction they rebel.

Certainly, there are times when parents, teachers and administrators must set limits for children without options. However, a discussion of why a situation occurred, along with the opportunity for the child to present his view, empowers him and leaves him feeling like a part of the resolution, rather than left out and controlled arbitrarily.

On the other hand, both authoritative warm and permissive warm parents sometimes err by letting discussions go on far too long. This is counterproductive. To be effective, a discussion, whether about a dilemma that a child faces or a situation that arises because of an infraction, must be succinct. Monitoring your parenting style will allow you to stay aware of your effectivness as a parent. Children raised in a permissive cold atmosphere receive very little parental guidance. At its worst, this style is characterized by a lack of concern, structure or foundation for security. A responsible child will still do the right thing, but it is risky. A permissive cold home can breed children who, left to their own devices, may neglect or harm themselves or feel little motivation to succeed.

CHILDREN HAVE FEARS

Anxious Feelings

Anxiety is unexpressed fear. Fears appear to be increasing among the children we see in our practices. An effective way to help your child deal with feelings of anxiety is to accept her fears as real. Provide reassurance and try these strategies:

- Acknowledge the fear
- Organize fears
- Prepare for emergencies

The result is empowerment.

Brandi saw a young girl professionally who was plagued by excessive fears. She asked her if she had any questions about her fears. The girl said, "Yes. I don't really understand why I'm scared, because I don't really know what I'm worrying about." Brandi explained that she had something called anticipatory anxiety. She worries ahead of time about various possible, but unlikely things, instead of feeling confident that if she got into a problematic situation, she would have the knowledge of what to do. Her states of anxiety and worry were constant.

Imagine yourself looking through a magnifying glass, where everything you see is enlarged. That is what happens with fears that are fact-based but excessively magnified.

In California, where people tend to fear earthquakes, one boy told Brandi he worried about earthquakes every time he rode the elevator up to her office. Brandi told him that she could not promise that there would never be an earthquake, but she was glad he asked because she could show him how she was prepared for one. She told him she had a radio, a key to the stairway, two flashlights and that she was aware of the best ways to leave the building. If anything happens, he knows she has thought ahead and prepared for an emergency. He seemed quite satisfied and relieved to have this information.

This approach of discussing a fear and adopting a plan applies to personal safety as well. We can never guarantee that something bad will not happen. One boy had his skateboard stolen by force while he was skating on a busy main street. Now every time he skateboards, he worries that it will be stolen again. He described his concerns:

"You know, it's the bad 'what ifs' which frighten me the most. I find myself asking bad 'what ifs' about everything. Whether I'm alone, attempting something new at school, or skateboarding on Melrose Avenue, I worry about bad possibilities."

Now he skates only on side streets. Brandi told him this was okay, that it is an adaptation.

Sometimes when there has been a traumatic event that triggers anxiety, it is important to allow for a time of recovery. This period may require a series of small steps that lead to overcoming the fear. This boy decided to skateboard because it was important to him to continue doing something that provided him with pleasure. He does not avoid skating; he just chooses to skate where he feels safe. Later, he may return to main streets, but only when he is ready.

Help your child understand that sometimes we are fearful, yet fear can be a productive emotion. Fears are like an alarm system in the body; when that alarm goes off, it makes us more alert to what is happening around us so we can do a better job of protecting ourselves.

Another practical method of helping a fearful child is to play or talk out, "What if?" A mother was speaking to her daughter about her fears, worries and anticipation. She suggested they talk about the worst things that could happen. If the worst happens, how will we handle it? What is the best strategy for dealing with it? If you had magical powers to change the situation, what would you do?

Playing "What if" allows even a young child to feel empowered. By encouraging her to anticipate alternatives and solutions, the focus turns positive and reduces the fear of disaster.

Media attention is often directed towards disasters. If your child exhibits fears, assure him that these are rare events; however, it is still a good idea to develop your own family emergency plan. Assigning emergency preparedness tasks to each family member can help alleviate fears. Make them age-appropriate; for example, your kindergartner can be in charge of placing a flashlight next to each bed, while your high school student can plan escape routes in case of fire.

Daily Strategies to Lessen Fears

Make your child aware of family plans ahead of time. When your child knows what to expect, they will be less fearful. Keep a chart listing activities for the week along with a family calendar, and review plans at bedtime or at the start of the day.

Visualize an event with a positive outcome. Role play an activity with a variety of scenarios. These techniques teach young children routines and help alleviate fears, such as:

- The dark
- Monsters
- Abandonment
- Things that might happen
- New situations
- Children's own imaginings
- Waking up from nightmares
- Drowning
- Snakes, dogs, other animals, insects and spiders
- Being left at school
- Being lost

Older children can be fearful too. Their fears include social issues, such as being disliked, being rejected and being ignored. In addition, they worry about:

- Failure or poor performance
- Earthquakes
- Fire
- Death
- Predators
- Physical attack
- Emotional attack
- Things they hear or see in newspapers or television news programs
- Current events

Reading stories that address fears can have a very powerful and calming effect on a child. We see many parents who use stories, such as *Where the Wild Things Are* by Maurice Sendak, to flush out their younger children's fears and promote discussion. Older children also respond to the power of story. Many public libraries have children's librarians, who are wonderful guides to stories that address these issues. Bookstores are wonderful resources for bibliotherapy help.

Worry vs. Wonder

An important distinction exists between worry and wonder. If you are wondering about something, then you are curious about it but not frightened by it. Worrying is more like going in a circle; it is ruminating, which is less productive than wonder because generally, it does not lead to a good outcome.

Heather defines "worry" as, "When you're crowded up and lonely all day, you can't think about anything else." Worry comes from fear and anticipatory anxiety. Worry has one possibility: that something bad is going to happen. Wonder makes room for all kinds of possibilities: I wonder how I did on that test? I wonder if I did better than I think I did? Did I do worse than I think I did?

Brandi often uses the phrase, "I was wondering about…" That implies thinking, which permits openness to what might happen without negative expectations. It is admitting that you care. A mother, who was extremely worried about her child's grade on a test,continued to discuss it at length. Looking at her daughter, she asked, "Are you worried about the test?" The daughter paused and then said, "No, Mom, I'm just wondering about it." Thinking about events can be useful as a way to expand understanding of a situation.

Brandi has a shrinking machine idea that has been a useful tool for many. Visualize the worry. Notice how it looms large in your imagination or as a visualization before your eyes. Now, shrink it down to a tiny size, as small as a speck. Each time a worry approaches say to yourself, "I can make this a tiny worry or I can choose another thought or action instead."

Some parents offer advice that implies a type of control no one can have: "Whatever you worry about will never happen. The things that you don't worry about are the things that will happen." The opposite is stated as, "If you worry about it, it won't happen." If you had only known to worry about the other things, they wouldn't have happened either.

High-achieving students who attribute their success to fear or worry have learned a false lesson. It is not worry that has made them successful but their ability to anticipate what needs to be done and then do it. Worry is the motivator, but it comes with a price. Unless we take an action, we will neither begin to be productive nor turn the obsessive thought to something achievable.

Anticipatory Anxiety

Like wonder, anticipatory anxiety can lead to a positive, successful experience, but it can also lead to the ultimate worry—procrastination. Some worriers spend their time worrying instead of just doing whatever has to be done. It may come from the worry that the product is not going to be good enough, so they never start. This may be a sign of perfectionism. The Serenity Prayer, which begins, "Give me the wisdom to accept the things I cannot change..." shows us that the key to coping with worry is through understanding that not everything can be fixed or made perfect.

Worry does its dirtiest work in the dark, and children in particular tend to worry at night. Offer your child a piece of paper or a tape recorder, so that if he wakes up or cannot sleep, he can make a tape of his worry or write a note about it. When we tell our concerns to someone else, they may suggest alternate ways to solve the problem. In addition, this will teach your child that when she brings a problem to the light and talks about it to other people, some of its power is immediately lost.

Another good technique for worriers is to create a worry list at the same day and time every week. For example, on Wednesday nights from 7:00 - 7:20, have your child write everything that he is currently worried about. With a young child, you can write it down for him. Then set an appointment for the following Wednesday to review the previous week's worry list and create a new one. You may create a column to the right of your worry list that includes any action steps you can think of to overcome the worry.

WORRIES	ACTION PLAN	DATE TO ACHIEVE	OUTCOME

EMPOWERMENT STRATEGIES FOR CHILDREN

Advice to Help Your Child In and Out of the Classroom

- Talk about things your child can do.
- Discuss the array of choices people have for education, work and life.
- Each of us is different and has a variety of talents, abilities and interests. Notice people who have adapted to their abilities and found ways to use them effectively.
- Identify fears and encourage your child to talk about them.
- Teach your child to have a sense of humor.
- Help your child reduce his expectations of teachers.

Actions Children Can Take to Increase Empowerment

- Help your family, friends and other people
- Think before acting
- Wait your turn
- Do not respond to rude people; walk away
- Encourage sensitive people
- Know when to intervene and when to step aside
- Always encourage, never tease
- Compliment others and accept compliments from others
- Notice other people's feelings
- Ponder
- Wonder
- Daydream
- Examine
- Try
- Say: "can," and "will"
- Compare, think, then decide
- Forgive some people; forget others
- Have hobbies, pursue interests, develop talents
- Take time to be quiet
- Play nicely
- Be a good sport
- Laugh often and hard

IN WHAT WAYS HAS RT/CT AFFECTED
OR CHANGED YOUR PERSONAL LIFE AND/OR
YOUR PUBLIC OR PROFESSIONAL LIFE?

- Show enthusiasm
- Show respect
- Show tolerance
- Stay aware of world events
- Read
- Write
- Value life
- Eat sensibly
- Get enough sleep
- Help yourself
- Exercise
- Be friendly
- Be generous in large and small ways
- Do not litter
- Be sincerely caring about others
- Open a door for someone
- Watch when you enter an elevator or doorway.
  If someone is exiting, step aside first, then enter.
- Smile
- Cry
- Be curious
- Ask questions
- Try something new

Winners and Losers

The difference between winners and losers is that winners tend to feel a sense of power and control. Losers attribute their success to the fact that a test was easy or a teacher feels sorry for them, whereas winners attribute success to the amount of effort they put into a task. Winners attribute failure to not having enough time to complete a task or not enough effort on their part, while losers attribute failure to being stupid or inadequate.

Motivation

Children give off warning signs when motivation declines. A backpack stuffed with graded papers, a dejected or defeatist attitude, failing grades or a dramatic change in grades are signs that a previously motivated student has lost momentum.

Your child may tell you, "I have no homework" when you know he does. Another warning sign can be a change in friendships, discarding high achieving friends and suddenly choosing new friends, who make little effort at school. Children, especially teens, drop out of a group with which they feel they cannot compete. Other warning signs include:

- Silence about what is happening at school or with their work
- Reluctance to want to talk about anything that is academically related
- Immersion in television, telephone, computer games

Do not be afraid to take advantage of external sources of information and bring them back to your child. For example, if another parent mentions a test of which you are unaware, tell your child you heard there was a history test. It would be natural to inquire about this topic out of curiosity.

Some schools give progress reports when a child starts to fail. If you have concerns, try the following suggestions:

- Call the school
- Become actively involved in your child's school program
- Avoid becoming a drill sergeant by quizzing your child the minute you pick him up from school

This problem can occur at any stage of learning—elementary, middle or secondary school. Many young students become unmotivated because they feel overwhelmed. Once these students feel the task is possible, their desire to achieve returns. We have witnessed students whose eyes light up with enthusiasm once they realize how to approach an assignment, which was previously viewed as "impossible." They grab for paper and pen. Sometimes this change will require the help of an educational therapist, a tutor or a psychologist.

Encouraging Creativity and Productivity

When your child is in the midst of creating something, you may unwittingly interfere with the process. For example, if you pass by when he is drawing a castle and remark, "That's a beautiful castle! I like the dragon..." the child will make a decision:

- He may decide to just keep on drawing with his own plan
- He may do something to please you and change the drawing
- Or, if the child has low self-esteem, he may cross out the castle and/or the dragon or tear up the drawing

What the compliment does is interfere with the creative process. Try to be courteous when your child is in the middle of a creative and/or imaginative effort. Here is the story of one over-eager parent's attempt to help her son—another example of how too much interference can destroy a wonderful learning experience.

Case Study: The summer before 7th grade, Adam's school sent home To Kill a Mockingbird for him to read. The assignment was to read the book and discuss it with his family. Adam's mother bought Cliff Notes, a book summary and made a list of 120 vocabulary words. Adam never read or discussed the book and relied on spoon-fed summaries. This is an example of a sure way to squeeze any joy out of what your child needs to discover for himself.

A crucial element in encouraging your child's motivation is to teach her to evaluate failure as useful information. By reviewing a test she brings home with a "D" or "F" grade, you can help her learn from her mistakes. Without further comment say, "Let's read over the test." Ask questions that help gather information rather than questions that will sound judgmental.

"Have you ever seen this kind of question before?" is an example of information gathering. "Did you do your homework?" implies judgment or accusation.

Once you determine on which parts of the test she did well, then ask, "What could you do next time if your next test looks like this?" "What could we do to make this better for you?" This process will generate a list of strategies that you can use to help your child become a motivated, more effective student.

In summary, empower your child by encouraging him to think of strategies to solve his problems. Whether he is worried about a new teacher, worried about grades or being accepted by friends or how to handle an emergency, you must acknowledge these worries and fears as real; then help him devise action plans to cope with and solve problems as they arise.

EMPOWERMENT ACTIVITIES

A. Go over the following list of actions with your child to empower him:

- Help people
- Think before acting
- Wait your turn
- Do not respond to rude people; walk away
- Avoid "toxic" people
- Encourage sensitive people
- Know when to intervene and when to step aside
- Never tease
- Compliment others and accept compliments from others
- Help your family and friends
- Address your feelings
- Notice other people's feelings
- Ponder
- Wonder
- Daydream
- Examine
- Try
- Say: "can," and "will"
- Compare, think, the decide
- Forgive some people, forget others
- Have hobbies
- Pursue interests
- Develop talents
- Take time to be quiet
- Play nicely
- Be a good sport
- Be passionate
- Show respect

- Show tolerance
- Help ignorant people
- Stay aware of world events
- Read
- Write
- Value life
- Eat sensibly
- Help yourself and others
- Be friendly
- Be generous in large and small ways
- Do not litter
- Be sincerely caring about others
- Open a door for someone
- Allow someone to enter an elevator or doorway first
- Smile
- Cry
- Laugh
- Be curious
- Ask questions
- Take measured risks
- Try something new

B. Make a list:

1. What are your concerns?

_____
_____
_____
_____
_____

2. What is your empowerment plan?

_____
_____
_____
_____
_____

NOTES:

CHAPTER 3

HOMEWORK AND USE OF TIME

Chapter Highlights

Gaining Time
Organization
Five Time Management Tips for Homework
Quality Time
Helping with Homework
Why is Homework Assigned?
How Much is Enough?
Three Helpful Steps to Take
Scheduling Homework
Tips for Parents to Make Homework Productive
Study Skills and Organization Hints
Note-Taking tricks for Students
Study Tricks
Prioritize
Backpack Privacy
Re-energize
Health Habits
Monitoring Progress
Where to Study in the House
Beat the Clock
Avoiding the Battle
Homework as a Symptom
Excuses, Excuses, Excuses
Whose Homework Is It?
Snack Time and Breaks
Bedtime and Sleep
Relaxation Exercises and Getting Ready for Bed
Starting the Next Day in a Pleasant Way

Lack of time is today's nemesis. We are so over-booked, over-programmed and over-involved, that private time and quiet time have become a luxury. Children have more access to computers, television, sports and projects than time to do them all. Over stimulation from too many activities makes it difficult for some children to settle into sleep. During the day, they may be anxious about their ability to compete or perform. In this chapter, we will suggest time management strategies that can lead to higher productivity and lessen anxiety.

Gaining Time

Many students complain of the pressure of completing all their homework while participating in extra-curricular activities. They say, "I'm not worried about managing time. I just wish I had more time to manage."

Recently, a high school sophomore wrote an English essay declaring her "Independence from Sleep." She argued that by eliminating sleep, she could fulfill her school responsibilities and still have time to read a book for pleasure, play tennis, and hang out with friends.

Our rapid pace of life interferes with our need for private time and adequate sleep. It is a privilege to have so many opportunities, but these activities crowd out the kind of leisure when people can decompress, relax, cool down, calm down and take the time to think, dream and imagine.

Significant research suggests that boredom presents an opportunity to daydream and for quiet time, when people can be most creative and can use the part of their brain that allows them to be inventive. Fantasy frequently leads to critical thinking skills and independence; therefore, when your child says she is bored, you do not have to feel compelled to spring into action and provide a project for her. Ask your child to give some thought to what she might like to do. Say, "Oh, how lucky, you are bored. Now you have some free time."

We recommend scheduling free time into your life and your child's life by setting aside family "quiet time" where everybody reads or writes or thinks or meditates. Later in the evening is often the best time for families to engage in this kind of unstructured activity.

Organization

There is a wonderful story about an old lady who was known for getting many things done and doing them well. When asked for the key to being so productive, the lady replied that she was a knitter. She said a knitter has to know where to find her needles and yarn, so she must always keep her materials in the same place. She needs to keep track of what she has already accomplished and what remains to be done, and she must plan before she acts.

Many of us could profit from this knitter's wisdom. A sense of accomplishment comes from grouping our materials together, knowing where we can find them, keeping track of our yarn so we know when we are about to run out, and having the pride of a project completed. Organizational skills require the ability to sequence and to plan ahead.

Five Time Management Tips for Homework

Establish a time management plan at the very beginning of the school year. This way, the whole family will understand that a specific time is set for homework, where your child will be studying, and the parameters of homework time. The family might make an effort to plan quiet activities with younger family members so your older child can focus on his studies. Review the plan on a regular basis, adjust and adapt it as schedules and needs change.

1. *Create a visual map of the week*. An activity for students of any age, who have tried to use calendars and student daily planners without success, is to create a visual map of the week. Purchase a corkboard and tack seven 3 x 5 cards across the top to represent the days of the week. (A white board with colored markers works well too.) Using a thick, black marker, write each assignment on a separate card. Next do a reverse task analysis as to the steps it takes to complete each assignment. For example, if there will be a spelling test on Friday, look back to Monday and ask if your child needs to do anything on Monday to prepare for the Friday spelling test. Perhaps by Tuesday, she will need to determine which words she knows and which need to be studied. Then skip Wednesday. On Thursday, do a final spelling review. At the end of the week, hold a ceremony by ripping up the cards or crossing out each step.

**Sample
Spelling Homework Chart**

Monday	Tuesday	Wednesday	Thursday	Friday
Make note of upcoming spelling test on Friday	Separate out and review unfamiliar words	Apply words to a story or sentences used in context	Final word review	Spelling test

It can be extremely helpful to actually see what is expected of you and how much time you have to complete each task. After mastering the map of the week technique, many students are then ready to make effective use of calendars and daily planners.

2. *Two-column note taking.* Recent research by vision specialists indicates that the eye scans more effectively vertically than horizontally. Trial lawyers have successfully used this note taking technique for generations. Check with college student stores for lined paper with an extra wide left margin for taking notes.

- Learn to take your notes in columns.
- Write down everything you hear in a wide right hand column.
- Attempt to write topics and main ideas in the left-hand column.
- Later, review your notes and put the main idea to the left of the matching detail.
- Connect ideas with colored pens and highlighters.
- Learn to use spaces between lines for main ideas.

3. ***Create a checklist.*** One of the most painful experiences in a student's life comes after she has worked hard on a project only to discover she has for gotten to pack it into her backpack and turn it in at school on time. To help prevent these heartaches, create a checklist (see sample below), which can be reviewed either the night before or the morning of school, *and check off each item.*

Put the checklist in a secure place so it is not one more thing to search for during the frantic rush to get out the door in the morning. Keeping the checklist with the backpack is helpful; some parents have gone so far as to laminate it and turn it into a luggage tag attached to the backpack, although some students do not want to be that obvious. You can keep the form readily accessible by the house exit door or next to the calendar, as long as it is visually available at all times.

Sample Checklist

OBJECT	CHECK OFF WHEN PACKED
TEXTBOOKS	
WORKBOOKS	
HOMEWORK	
LUNCH	
SNACK	
MONEY (LUNCH/PHONE/EMERGENCY)	
JACKET	
SCHOOL SUPPLIES (PENS, PENCILS, ETC.)	
SPECIAL EVENTS SUPPLIES	
FORMS TO BE RETURNED	
MISCELLANEOUS	

4. ***The Backpack.*** Organization of the backpack is crucial. Ideally, everything should be easy to find. You may want to rehearse with your child and say, "When you open your backpack at school, what is the first thing you are going to do?" Agree on a plan with your child about what happens if something is left behind. Are you willing to bring it to him at school? Are there any consequences for him if it is left behind?

5. ***When assignments are left at home.*** Organizational ability varies among children. Some children have a problem with organization, planning ahead and following through. They frequently leave things behind and torture their parents with frantic phone calls about missing lunch boxes, homework, papers, etc. In that case, it may be best not to take those items and let it be a lesson in organization and planning. Even though being rescued can produce a truly wonderful feeling in a child there may be times when you are not able to perform that rescue because of your work schedule or other demands in your life. Be clear about the policy and about your own limitations ahead of time.

Quality Time

Is it true that giving your child quality time is better than large quantities of time? For years, social researchers have studied the issue without a definitive answer. Our observations, however, lead us to conclude that quality time is overrated and abused. Some people use the term quality time when families go to an event together, shop together, or have lunch together. For young children and even adolescents, there is enormous value just in being in your child's presence.

There is value to just being able to say to your child, "I'm working on this now, but in ten minutes I will come in and we will read that chapter together. I will quiz you on your history. We will play Scrabble." Your child knows, more powerfully than with words, how important he is to you.

One woman, who thought of herself as a highly involved parent, was very active in the PTA and charitable organizations. She said she made sure she spent "quality time" with her children, but in truth, she spent three out of the five school nights going to meetings. Her children began having homework problems and expressing unhappiness and dissatisfaction with school. Someone suggested to this involved mom that she just stay home rather than going to three meetings a week. When she reduced her schedule to an average of one meeting a week, it provided a subtle but powerful change for her family.

Helping with Homework

HOMEWORK STINKS, by Lauren

"After a long hard day of school, homework is the last thing that I want to do. I wake up every morning at 6:30. I have to be in school at 7:30. Then I go to school until 3:30, counting down the minutes. When I get home, the last thing I want is more work. Paragraphs for English; reading, then answering questions for history; projects for science; health articles for P.E., and then at least 20 problems for math! By the time I finish, it's time to go back to school!! So in conclusion, it is evident that homework is a waste of time!"

All students benefit from their parents' help; this fact is even truer for children with learning differences. Mark Griffin, Ph.D., Chairman of the National Center for Learning Disabilities' (NCLD) Professional Advisory Board and founding headmaster of a school for the learning disabled in Greenwich, Connecticut, had this to say:

"Parents who become involved in how a child studies are more likely to discover whether the child has a learning disability and to provide the support the youngster needs to achieve success in school."

Please remember that providing help is quite different from actually doing a child's homework. We encourage parents to assist with the when, where and how of homework, but not do the actual work itself.

Why is Homework Assigned?

There are many purposes for homework. We have listed some here:

◆ Homework extends the learning from the school day, enhances what has been learned, and reinforces and solidifies the learning. It is an opportunity for children to practice what they have learned that day.

◆ Homework can teach responsibility and independence. It gives the child the opportunity to take on an assignment and follow through.

◆ Homework allows the teacher an opportunity to gauge how the student is actually doing, which concepts they understand and which need more time or work.

◆ Homework is good for the parent, too. A little of the school is brought home. Once the parent gets a sense of what the homework is about, the parent has a greater understanding of what the child is working on at school. An informed parent spots problems and helps find solutions.

How Much Is Enough?

Some parents hold the view that if a school gives a significant amount of homework, it is a better school. Homework should be comprised only of the amount of material that reinforces learning and concepts, as listed above. If the child cannot do the homework independently, then the parent may need to assist. If that need becomes excessive, it may mean that parents or their representatives have to step in to discuss with the teacher whether the assignments are appropriate.

Matthew started sixth grade in a new school and was so overwhelmed by the amount of homework he was assigned that he refused to do it. We spoke with Matthew's teacher and arranged that he complete every odd-numbered problem of his homework for the next few weeks. This gave Matthew a sense that his homework was manageable. Ironically, by the second night he was able to do all the even numbered problems in five minutes. This simple technique gave Matthew the sense that it was possible to complete his work and it relieved his feelings of frustration and fear.

In elementary school, take a look at your child's work. Are there eighteen problems that are all the same? Would nine sufficiently reinforce the concept for your child? Is this the consistent pattern in homework? You may want to present this issue at a parent-teacher conference. If other parents have mentioned this same concern, encourage them to present the same issue in a friendly, informative way to the teacher. If there is not enough feedback on homework, bring it up at full parent-teacher meetings, such as a PTA meeting and/or talk to the administrators.

Many middle school and high school students report missing after-school activities because of excessive homework. They can no longer play on the soccer team. They must give up dance lessons because they do not have time to finish their homework. An important question for the parents is whether homework and study time are balanced among classes. Find out if the school makes up an official master calendar? Are all tests on Friday? What is the spacing of assignment and tests?

Occasionally, you will find your child in a school setting where the homework is much greater than you or your child ever thought it would be. Once you get past the shock, we have some suggestions to help you through the process.

Three Helpful Steps to Take

1. Sit down with your child and evaluate his ability to complete the assignments. Some children can handle huge amounts of schoolwork. Other children find it causes anticipatory anxiety, exasperation and excess worry.

2. Some middle schools and high schools will give out an assignment sheet in advance. If your child is willing to spend weekend time getting work done for the upcoming week, it is amazing how much pressure can be relieved.

3. If the homework is excessive, it is important to set a meeting with the teacher first, and, if necessary, with the school administrators to see what can be done. Discuss school policy toward homework, your concerns about its being excessive, and, most importantly, explain how the excessive work affects your child.

Scheduling Homework

To prevent a homework disaster, prioritize. Some children need to be highly scheduled and highly organized. Other children can pace themselves. Some children will take too long on one topic and not long enough on another. First, write out a schedule for the day using the Visual Map of the Week technique. Look at the assignments and help your child make a plan for the afternoon and evening, and estimate what is required for each assignment. Then write down blocks of time, with five minute breaks in between, say 4:00-4:15, 4:20-4:35.

Be sure the plan breaks the homework down into manageable chunks of work. This is crucial for the well being of your child. Once your child sees that schoolwork is manageable, she will no longer be intimidated by homework.

Before making the schedule, be sure to ask your child what is due the next day, what is due in the longer term and what tests are coming up. This way, your child can take test preparation time into account, as well as organize the assignments due the next day. What you do for your child by asking what is due the next day is to teach her how to prioritize. By modeling your behavior, your child will learn how to prioritize time and become an effective student.

Some children resist "reporting" their schedules. They might prefer having a written agenda or homework diary for your review. Others would rather be left alone. If you have confidence that your child is proceeding well independently, relax and allow this independence.

**SAMPLE
HOMEWORK SCHEDULE**

4:00	4:15	4:30	5:00	5:30	6:00	7:00	8:00
Snack	Bike ride or	math & science or	social studies or	study or	eat dinner	finish-home-work	get ready for bed
	relax or watch TV	test prep	English	help prepare dinner		clean-up	

Tips for Parents to Make Homework Productive

Studying in an organized and smart way requires practice. There are children who feel they must study everything, so they over-study, making endless note cards for every history test. You can help them create priorities and help them figure out what is important for a particular assignment and what is not by picking out the essential details.

Some students are self-starters while others need to know an adult is close by in order to do their best work. Take time to be near your child if she is the type who needs that.

Parents often lose patience when they tutor their children. Avoid statements such as, "You aren't getting this because you aren't trying. You don't want to learn. You're lazy. Why aren't you getting this through your head?"

Remember that children get frustrated; when they get mad and stomp off, that's the time for a break. Tell your child, "We need a break now. We'll try again after awhile."

Here are some tips:

- Show an interest in your child's homework.

- Coach your child on an unknown word or difficult problem, but let the child do the work.

- Help your child learn to make good decisions and understand limits. This can begin with when and where to do the homework.

- Establish a regular homework time.

- Find a special location in the house for your child to do homework.

- Eliminate as many distractions as possible during study time. Turn off the television. Turn on the telephone answering machine. Eat a snack before the homework begins. Be sure to ask siblings to respect this quiet time. Make use of earplugs, if necessary.

- Some children do benefit from background noise or "white noise" such as a fan or normal daily activities of the household. "Can I listen to music while I do my homework?" For some, Mozart and Bach seem to help them concentrate. Experimentation with new age music shows it may foster creative writing, by freeing the left side of the brain and Bach may enhance math performance. For most students, music with too clearly a defined lyric or beat will truly distract and we recommend that it not be encouraged.

- If a child strongly dislikes or has trouble completing the homework, find out why. This may signal an area of study that needs reinforcement. If the trouble persists, look further. Evaluate learning styles and be on the lookout for possible learning difficulties.

- Carefully observe your child's study habits and discuss them with his teachers.

♦   Try to relate the homework to the child's everyday life. For instance, if fractions and measurements are being studied, have the child prepare a favorite food using the different measurements.

♦   Praise your child for successfully completing homework. Nothing builds self-esteem like praise from parents.

♦   During study breaks, allow your child to play with toys or a pet, or chat with a parent, sibling or pal. During study hour, teach your child to attend and focus. For example, set a timer for twenty minutes to a half-hour of concentrated study time; then break for five to ten minutes and return to study. Encourage eating only on breaks or at set times, and avoid using food as a reward.

♦   Distinguish with your child what is considered a break and what is playtime. Fifteen-minute snacks, getting something to drink, stretching, checking in on family members or playing with the dog are examples of breaks. Many children choose television as a break, saying it rests their brain, but establish a clear policy on this. If the program lasts more than half an hour, avoid the battle by agreeing ahead of time that the break will only allow for watching part of the show but the rest will be taped. (If your child resists getting back to work when the show is only half over, you have the option of limiting or suspending television privileges.)

Study Skills and Organization Hints

Organization is a critical factor in student success. The following ideas and study hints may be of value to your child in enhancing study skills, organization or completion of homework.

♦   Acquire an organizer book with a simple structure to help with daily planning of assignments and appointments. Data can either be handwritten or maintained on a computer with an organizer program.

♦   Keep your backpack orderly.

♦   Purchase an indexed three-ring binder or separate folders for each class.

◆ Gather everything you need in one place before you go to bed.

◆ Make notes of what you need to do in the morning.

◆ Maintain a calendar, and record test dates and due dates.

◆ Keep the family aware of changes in schedules.

Note-Taking Tricks for Students:

◆ Learn to type correctly as soon as possible. Keyboarding rapidly increases speed and accuracy as compared to handwriting. Some children are ready to begin keyboarding skills by third grade; others are not ready until eighth grade.

◆ Use a laptop computer to take notes in class. It is a faster method and allows greater flexibility for editing notes later. This can help the high school student take tests too.

◆ If your child's teacher permits, tape record lectures. This enables the student who has difficulty with writing speed to accurately review what was said. To eliminate any disruption from changing tapes during class, insert 120-minute tapes.

◆ Use highlighters to underline important information, instructions and directions. Underline key words and phrases.

◆ Reread directions, clarify instructions, and check your understanding of the assignments. Reread and proofread all your work.

◆ Purchase a pencil grip, which helps to encourage a tripod grip (with thumb and first finger pinching the pencil, middle finger resting underneath.) Hard pencil pressure causes the hand to fatigue and reduces writing speed. Grips are inexpensive and can be purchased at stationary or learning supply stores.

◆ Make it a habit to skip lines between subjects.

Study Tricks

Divide the assignment into steps and make a list of tasks for each day. (You can use the reverse-task analysis techniques previously described.) For example:

Monday	Read the text
Tuesday	Take notes, outline the subject, and prepare note cards
Wednesday	Write test questions
Thursday	Reread. Review and correct
Friday	Turn in the assignment

Prioritize

♦ List tasks, putting the least interesting and/or most difficult ones first and the easiest and/or most interesting last. Complete the difficult tasks first.

♦ Schedule relaxation time and commit to an appropriate time to return to the project.

♦ Identify and know your own pace. Set realistic goals to ensure success and complete assignments on time. If you tend to procrastinate, start early.

♦ Make a plan for accountability about work assignments and responsibilities at home. Write them down and check them off as they are done.

♦ If easily distracted, create personal cues to increase persistence. For example, write a "pay attention" reminder on Post-It notes. Make up a secret code word on a Post-It that means attention and concentration. Each time your attention wanders make a check mark.

♦ Plan rewards to encourage progress and motivation. Change the rewards as needed. Work towards internal pride in accomplishing the assignments.

Backpack Privacy

Do parents have the right to look through their child's backpack? It depends on the child's age and circumstance. We recommend that parents and students go through their backpacks together every day or at least once a week depending on the child. Call it Backpack (or Book Bag) Treasure Hunt. Backpack treasures have included prehistoric lunches, lost assignments, important notes to parents, notes the parents thought had been delivered to the school or teacher, notices of special school functions and meetings that are long past.

One school sent home a bulletin of the school events every Monday, yet a parent at that school was astounded to discover half way through the semester that she had missed several important events because she never got the bulletins. Sometimes, the child misses out:

Amy comes home in tears and says, "I couldn't go on the field trip because I didn't have a permission slip." "Why not?" the parent asks. It turns out that the permission slip had been living in the backpack for many weeks.

Your child can designate the day for Backpack Treasure Hunt, preferably Monday. Learn to do this together. Make it a weekly ritual and take a full five minutes. Remember that you are modeling organizational behavior for your child.

Be sure your child keeps an assignment book, an ongoing log of the assignments given and a system of checking off what is completed. Keep a reserve notebook for all materials and past notes that no longer need remain in the primary notebook your child takes to school every day. Use the reserve notebook to review for finals and tests. This has the added benefit of lightening the weight of the backpack.

Many orthopedists complain about the weight of backpacks. They suggest that backpacks be carried high and balanced between the shoulders or preferably in front, close to the body. Check into purchasing or renting an extra set of textbooks, one for school and one for home to lighten the backpack. Backpacks on wheels are available.

Re-Energize:

The following techniques can help relax and re-energize a distracted or tired student during study time:

- Uncross your legs, square your shoulders and sit up straight.

- 7-11 method. Breathe in through the nose to the count of seven and exhale through the mouth to the count of eleven. This is an exaggerated sigh, which can be very relieving emotionally.

- Using your palm, gently cup your eyes, focus on breathing, and visualize a special place, (e.g. the beach.) It takes as little as sixty seconds to feel calm.

- A moment of playing ball easily, riding an exercise bike slowly or jumping rope can make a difference for refocusing.

Health Habits:

- Get enough rest
- Eat properly
- Have fun when you can
- Enjoy learning and studying

Monitoring Progress:

We believe it is important that both students and parents attend school progress meetings. The student should attend in order to be involved with the process and to be accountable for the outcome, as well as to plan courses of action, to participate in creating goals, and to make decisions.

It is essential to identify realistic commitments, and establish accountability. For example, if your child fails to turn in homework regularly, have her start by turning in whatever she has done, even if only partially completed. Although the ultimate goal is completion, on the way to this goal, she can turn in whatever part is finished; however, each time another partial assignment is turned in, a greater percentage should have been completed than for the previous assignment.

Where to Study in the House

Whenever possible, designate one study area in the house. A few children can successfully study at the kitchen table in the center of other activity, because they need the sense that they are part of the action and not isolated from the rest of the family. Most children, however, need a private space, such as their bedroom, and they benefit from proper lighting, minimum noise and plenty of room to lay out books and papers. If possible, give them an organized desk. For those who study on the bed or on the floor, a lapboard will help them maintain more correct posture and reduce fatigue.

If your child is lucky enough to have a designated study area but is having trouble concentrating on the task or getting started, have him leave that area immediately. Stand up, stretch, walk around, think things through, but do not sit at that area. When he is then ready to work, have him go back to that area. You want your child to build an association between productivity and the designated study area, and this kind of pairing will help your student become more productive.

Beat the Clock

An old-fashioned technique for getting homework done quickly is to set a timer and say, "See how many of these problems you can do before the buzzer rings. If you can get this assignment done before the buzzer goes off, take an extra five minute break."

One parent said, "I am going to set the timer and do my work for 30 minutes while you do yours. At the end of that time, we will take a break together." It is a nice way to enjoy special time and yet have uninterrupted study time in a 30-minute block.

Avoiding the Battle

Homework battles between parents and children can be avoided by using the following techniques and sticking to these five rules:

1. Respect you child's integrity. Some parents insist on checking their child's homework even when it has been completed to their child's satisfaction. If your child independently completes homework and gets good feedback from her teacher, do not intrude. One child told us his father habitually made him correct small errors on his homework. His teacher did not think these minor errors were worth the time for correction. This boy began to hide his homework from his father, fearing he would have to redo all his homework every school night.

2. When your child asks for help, teach her to be specific in what to ask for. For example, encourage a request such as, "Can you help me with the steps of long division?" Help your child rephrase requests that are self-defeating, such as, "I'm too stupid to (or I can't) figure this out. You've got to help me."

3. Set a time limit for homework. Obviously, there will be exceptions, but generally stick to an agreed upon amount of time. We have met with too many families who have lost all concept of family time. For many, homework has become a family industry of excessive proportion. The following chart lists suggested daily amounts of time for homework:

GRADE	TIME LIMIT
Kindergarten	10 minutes (preferably none)
1st & 2nd	20 minutes
3rd & 4th	30-40 minutes
5th & 6th	1 hour
7th & 8th	1-2 hours
9th thru 12th	2-4 hours

4.   If your child wants you to review the homework, note possible corrections. Now for the truly challenging part! If at all possible, refrain from insisting upon corrections. This is your child's homework, not yours. Here is an opportunity to encourage autonomy and decision-making. When parents camouflage their children's learning deficits with perfect homework, it prevents the teacher from accurately assessing how best to help the child.

5.   Final step—turn it in! Sometimes the battle is not in doing the homework but in turning it in. Help your child picture herself turning in her homework.

Occasionally, we see cases where a child works very hard to complete her homework, but magically forgets to turn it in or leaves it in her desk or backpack. Teachers experience many instances during parent conferences where they open the desk of a child and find the completed homework that was never turned in. When the child was asked why this happened, excuses such as "I forgot" are offered.

Exploring the reasons for why this occurred are usually revealing. The student may not have taken pride in his work or felt that it was not well done. The perfectionist child is never satisfied. It could result from a failure to accept or understanding the responsibility. Sometimes a child truly forgets.

Homework as a Symptom:

Before fifth grade, children need understanding and guidance about the process of homework. At fifth grade, if not earlier, a child can take the responsibility of bringing homework to the teacher. Responsibility means:

- Complete the task
- Review the steps of homework
- Write down the assignment
- Bring it home
- Set aside time to finish it
- Have it reviewed by a parent (optional)
- Turn it in

Sometimes students do not turn in homework because they are keeping a secret; namely, that they cannot do the assignment. A client remembered that as a seventh grader, he managed not to turn in a single piece of written work. He knew his writing skills were unacceptable; and rather than proving that, he decided not to turn anything in. He was eventually referred for services to remediate his problem.

It is common for some children to hold secrets and not reach out for help. It is just as common for some parents to get impatient and to misunderstand instead of teaching their children more effective homework strategies.

CASE STUDY: The mother of fifth grader, "Perfect Angie," came to school for a parent conference ready to hear glowing reports about her daughter. The teacher, who assured her that Angie was a lovely girl, was puzzled because Angie had not turned in any homework for the last eight weeks. Mother became angry because the teacher had not notified her earlier. She was also disappointed in her daughter.

On impulse, she asked to see Angie's desk. Lifting the cover, they were surprised to discover a mass of jumbled papers shoved inside. As they struggled through the mess, they found all of Angie's completed homework. This was a symptom of Angie's difficulty with organization and long-term planning. She had always done well with assignments which were given one day and due the next; her fifth grade teacher was the first to give assignments with a variety of due-dates at the beginning of the week. Now Angie was lost.

This case exemplifies how a great kid can fall through the cracks, not know how to get out of the problem and end up feeling very bad about herself. Luckily, both Angie's teacher and her mother saw this discovery as an opportunity to teach Angie how to do advance planning and how to organize.

Excuses, Excuses, Excuses

Excuses that have been used to delay homework (or to avoid doing it) are:
- "The copy store was closed."
- "I am too tired."
- "It's too hard."
- "You weren't available to help me."
- "I'm sick."
- "It got stolen/I lost it/I forgot it."
- "We don't get credit for it, it's just practice."
- "It's not due until next week."
- "The teacher said that I know this so well I don't need to do the homework."
- "My Mom took it to work."
- "My dog ate it."
- "My computer crashed."
- "The computer wouldn't print my disk."

We have witnessed a curious phenomenon recently. There are children who resist doing their homework because they have a high need to exert their own will and maintain control over situations. It is helpful to recognize that they may want more quality time with a parent or time to play or be free. Negotiation may help them feel in control. If a child is adamant or being outrageous, try responding with one or more of the following sentences:

- Thank you for that viewpoint.
- That's an interesting idea. I'll give it some thought.
- I'll ponder that and think about what that means.

- ◆ You are welcome to be outrageous (trash-talk, play video games, resist homework, etc.) for the next three minutes, then return to being serious and sincere in your efforts.
- ◆ Nevertheless, teach your child to use "I can/I will" answers. I am tired so <u>I will</u> finish after dinner, (after a nap, in the morning.) <u>I will</u> try. Please help me with...<u>I can</u> do the rest on my own. My work was lost so <u>I will</u>... The dog ate it, so <u>I will</u> do it over.

Whose Homework Is It?

Recently, a fifth grade student won an award for a written essay. The parents and child readily admitted her father had edited and rewritten her essay. How does that child feel when she gets up on the stage and receives "her" award? Who should be getting the award?

One parent was concerned about having her child's tutor type a report, which the student dictated. The student felt as if the work was done <u>for</u> him. In this case, dictation was appropriate because in an evaluation of that boy's learning style, we had identified that he needed help in expression of his own thoughts and that he was learning-delayed in motor skills and writing. Dictating his report gave him an opportunity to practice his strength (verbal skills) and see results without extra hours of laboring over producing legible writing.

Snack Time and Breaks

Some children do not require snacks and breaks. They automatically take a stretch break and go right back to their task. Other children need to have a schedule of when to stretch, when to take a break and when to have a healthy snack.

Homework often becomes an endurance contest. Help your child plan her afternoon as an athlete prepares for an athletic event. Fuel up, warm up, pace yourself, perform and keep a positive attitude.

Plan breaks to communicate with another student by phone or via e-mail. Having a study buddy is helpful even for older students, but this works only if both students agree to talk a specified amount of time. Arrange schedules to talk together at a fixed hour, such as 8 o'clock and use timers if necessary.

Bedtime and Sleep

Although the amount of sleep each child needs can vary, it is imperative for each child to get enough sleep. Help your child go to bed on time and with ease. No amount of time management or study tricks will compensate for the powerful effects of fatigue due to incomplete sleep the night before. Many children come to school tired. They are often labeled with attention deficit disorder when, in some cases, the true disorder is sleep deprivation.

Getting a child to sleep can be a major challenge. By the end of the day, many parents are tired and desperate for a little quiet time. Children are tired, too but they may also be wound up. Often they do not know how to bring the energy level down and let go of the day. One weak strategy is to wait until your child is so exhausted that all you have to do is scoop them up from where they fall and place them into bed. Another poor technique is for parents to become so offensive, screaming and yelling about going to bed, that out of self- defense, your child goes to bed to stop hearing you yell. There are better methods.

Many parents ask us for help in easing the bedtime battles. Bewildered, they ask us: "This was not a problem when we were children, was it? Why is this such a huge problem now?" Fatigue can be a factor. Some children fight to stay awake, which comes from a natural childhood response at the thought of missing something or not wanting to give up the day. Bedtime, the moment when a child must let go of the day, leave the family environment and go to bed, can be a discussion, though not necessarily a negotiation. Bedtime limits need to be imposed, and sometimes, it takes a parent's willingness to assert authority to make this happen.

Set a clear bedtime. With the older child, you can negotiate about the hour, saying, "Now that you are in the second grade, I think 8:00 is a good time." Your child may negotiate for 8:15. You could agree that if the child shows that she can be in bed with lights out by the set time, fine; but if she is not sticking to the bargain by the end of the week, you will set bedtime back to 8:00. Write down the agreed upon bedtime rituals including reading together, chatting together, bathroom routines and getting ready for bed routines.

Relaxation Exercises and Getting Ready for Bed

Some children get very wound up over homework with no time to cool down before bed. Both parents and children can learn, practice and successfully use relaxation techniques.

A family we know plays games as a source for relaxation. Every night at nine o'clock, one family member chooses checkers or gin rummy. It sounds as if it would take a long time but this family ritual takes only a few minutes. It brings the family together and is more positive than repeatedly telling your child to relax and calm down. These small rituals can change the rhythm and pattern of the day before bedtime.

One of the most powerful points in your child's day can be those last few minutes before your child goes to sleep. It is also the time of the day when the parent is tired and the child is tired, but what message do you want to send in those last five minutes before your child goes to sleep? This is a time when children will express a worry, talk about a joy or tell you the things they would never tell you in the car coming home from school.

Therefore, it is a good time to make yourself available to just listen and have quiet time together. The tired parent may feel tempted to run out of the room, but here is where you define yourself as a listener and a parent with empathy. Stretch yourself. Take those extra moments to tune in to your child.

The following is a list of bedtime techniques that we have suggested to parents over the years:

♦ *Create a bedtime routine.* Pretend you are a kind drill sergeant in the army to make the ritual the same each night. If someone wants to change the routine, have a family meeting to discuss it. List a future date to try the new procedure.

♦ *Undertake a transition activity.* After homework is done, have your child play a game that is not too physical, then have a bath and follow up with a short story.

- *Review of the day.* Some children have a hard time letting go of the day. You may need to guide them through a step-by-step review of their day. Ask, "What is the first thing you did today? What did you do after that?" For some children, you may have to take notes so they can see that it is all written down. This is a simple but highly effective technique for letting go of "running" or persistent thoughts. This allows relaxation to begin.

- *Create your own relaxation tape.* Contracting and releasing muscles as you move up the body from the toes is a traditional relaxation technique. This technique is enhanced when your child records the commands, so he can listen to a tape of his own voice guiding him through the muscle contraction and relaxation. Some of our clients have gotten very creative with this exercise and have included music, bells, and or nature sounds in the tapes.

- *Play a commercial relaxation tape.* Many are available. Choose an environmental sound tape that is soothing.

- *Install a night-light.* For younger children, put one in the bathroom or bedroom to make the room feel safe. Try to avoid leaving the room light on.

- *Make plans of action.* Some children get preoccupied with worry about the next day and what is coming up on the weekend. Write an agenda for the weekend or write an agenda for the next day so that the child can feel secure with the plan.

Starting the Next Day in a Pleasant Way

Some children arise in a cheerful mood and with ease. Other children find getting up in the morning a challenge. They act tired. They are not helpful. They avoid eating breakfast. They complain about their body aches. They generally look miserable. These children need loving care from a parent who is willing to set limits and boundaries. Give your child warnings and inform her about what your specific expectations are for the morning.

Despite the fact that we are not fans of punishment, restrictions may be appropriate for a difficult morning child. The duration should be one or two days, not a sentence of weeks of punishment. Encourage the child to arise the next morning a bit more cheerful. If your child has a hard time getting up in the morning to go to school, make sure she is getting enough rest.

It helps to prepare a difficult child the night before by saying to her to try her best to wake up in the morning when her alarm rings or when the parent awakens her. Tell your child that if she would like five minutes more to sleep, she needs to notify you. She must arise without complaining, dress properly, lay out clothes the night before, organize the backpack, have breakfast, greet the family, show up for carpool or leave for school on time. Otherwise, privileges such as television, computer time or play time that evening will be lost. The child will then need to write a note or express a plan for the next day to help understand that this is her responsibility, not the parent's responsibility.

Starting the day by racing around, fighting or arguing creates anxiety in children and causes them to start the day with resistance and feeling upset. To start the day cheerfully means that everyone starts off on a good foot instead of with a worry or a conflict.

Children's needs and parents' expectations change with each stage in a child's development. Most important is accountability. Please always remember to ask your child what she plans to do to improve. The reason for trying to improve the way a child behaves is that she becomes accountable and responsible for her own behavior.

NOTES:

CHAPTER 4

GRADES AND TAKING TESTS

Chapter Highlights

GRADES

Report Cards and Progress Reports
When Do Grades Count?
Academic Probation
Grade Inflation
Parent Reaction
Good Grades
Peer Competition, Pressure to Perform and Incentives
Children's Reactions
Incentives
Action Plans

TESTS

Testing skills
Preparing for a Test
Test-Taking Strategies and Test Anxiety
Strategies for Test Preparation
Retaking Examinations
Professional Resources

The purpose of education is to teach students to become independent critical thinkers. In this competitive world it is easy to lose sight of that purpose and to focus on grades and report card remarks. Nevertheless, grades are commonly used both to measure progress and to convey this information to parents, students and institutions. In this chapter, we will address various challenges that arise around grades. We will also discuss aspects of a related issue—testing—and offer suggestions that can help you and your child approach both issues calmly.

GRADES

Report Cards and Progress Reports

Not all children care about their grades. Some students work harder than others to earn higher grades; they know what it takes to get an "A" and they work toward that goal. Other students know what it takes to get a "B" and limit their efforts to that level because they are satisfied with less. Still others lack the academic capability to earn an "A" or "B" grade.

When children are asked to give reasons why they should try hard in school, they offer responses such as:

- "So I can get good grades."
- "So I can get into a good college."
- "So I will not stay back and can move up to the fifth grade."
- "So my Mom and Dad will buy me presents."
- "Because my parents expect me to."

WORKBOOK: Ask your child their reasons for wanting to get good grades. Record their responses here.

Answers:

_____

_____

_____

_____

After discussing positive reasons for working hard, excelling in school and earning good grades, write a new list with more positive goals.

_____

_____

_____

_____

_____

Typically, schools issue report card grades four times per year, but the grades that count toward a cumulative record are the ones given at the end of each semester. The interim report cards usually are called progress reports.

Some schools send progress reports to let parents know that a student is in danger of getting a poor grade or is doing exceptionally well and making great progress. Find out what reporting system your school uses and when reports and grades are issued.

Traditional report cards indicate progress with letter grades. Reports on cooperation and study habits (citizenship) may also appear. Some report cards include an anecdotal message from the teacher. Increasingly, we see schools using a form that avoids traditional grades and only gives an anecdotal report. These reports may indicate only if the student is on grade level (satisfactory), needs improvement, or is outstanding.

Parents commonly report to us that they experience difficulty interpreting the information on an anecdotal report. Many teachers are overly concerned about children's self-esteem so they issue glowing reports, which mask areas of difficulty. We have heard parents say, "My child is in third grade, still not reading, but you would never know it to read this report." Sometimes it takes a professional to look for certain key words or phrases in the report to get a true picture of how the child is functioning in the classroom. Look for phrases such as:

- "Is a leader but leads in his own direction"
- "Is a lovely child but has difficulty staying with the group"
- "Is improving in..."
- "Has shown growth in..."
- "Is making progress"

When parents read a report card, they should write down their questions and ask them at the next parent-teacher conference. We suggest that parents call the teacher immediately and approach the appointment from the standpoint of information gathering, not as a competition or an attack. Ask the teacher what his words mean? Use phrases such as "At home I see my child... How do you see him at school? I do not see him doing his homework. He does not seem to care what his work looks like. While he sounds highly motivated, he does not seem to care."

Social development usually is addressed on a report card as well. A comment on the report card indicating that your child is accepted and liked by his classmates is encouraging; however, if your child is rarely invited for play dates or birthday parties, ask the teacher for specific examples of his acceptance by his schoolmates. Perhaps the child is quiet, somewhat withdrawn but not creating any behavioral disturbances for the teacher. Do not forget to ask your child who his special friends are and with whom he plays. Have that information ready when you speak with the teacher.

Do not be surprised if you gain new information at the parent-teacher conference. It is often easier for teachers to share examples in a comfortable face-to-face setting than writing these comments in a formal report.

When Do Grades Count?

Grades count when they are part of admission to the next educational step or admission to the next school.

Elementary School:

Grades become important by the fourth grade when a minimum grade-point average is required to move on to academically competitive middle schools (and later to high schools). This is very important to students who will be applying to private secondary schools. This does not mean that grades from the early years should not be taken seriously. They are an important indication of how your child is progressing.

Coming from a school where letter grades are not given can create a problem when a child tries to transfer. Some of these schools have a system where, in addition to the anecdotal information, they record the student progress as on grade level, above grade level or needs improvement. This enables the next school to gauge how your child performs in comparison with his classmates.

Middle School:

Middle school grades are an indicator of your child's adjustment to and performance at a large school multi-class setting. Although middle school grades are not part of the transcript sent to colleges, some students must apply to high school after the eighth grade. Their grades in the sixth and seventh grades become important as criteria for selection.

High School:

The importance of grades in high school is a topic of debate. Some college admissions officers stress grade point average, while others strongly support the concept that the grade point average is not as important as the difficulty of the classes the student has taken.

Case Study: A student, who graduated from a private high school with a 4.0 GPA (grade point average), was denied admission to the college of her choice. A fellow student with a lower GPA was accepted. The difference between these two students was that the first student had chosen her classes based on subjects in which she could get her best grades. In the interest of higher grades, she avoided honors classes and AP classes and dropped all outside activities. This resulted in her appearing as a candidate who was unwilling to strive. The second girl struggled through honors classes but chose them because the subjects were of great interest to her. She had also established a babysitting referral service at age twelve. The college chose to invest in the student who took risks and followed her interests.

Each college configures the high school grade point average differently. Many state universities and colleges use grade point averages and SAT (Scholastic Aptitude Test) scores as the only factors for admission, although this may change. Private colleges typically consider many other factors. Therefore, high school students must consider the grade profile he needs to present in his college applications.

Academic Probation

If your child attends private school, expect to receive a contract for the following academic year. However, if you receive a letter saying your child may not be invited back and has been placed on academic probation, an investigation and prompt action are required.

Some schools regularly send out these letters. Although they need not be taken too seriously, it is absolutely essential that you immediately make a phone call to your child's advisor, counselor, administrator, head of school and teacher to schedule a meeting to determine what is necessary to remove the academic probation status. Be sure your child is present at that meeting.

Arrive with pen and paper, and if it will not create conflict, bring a tape recorder. Find out exactly what is required of your child to remain in school. This is the crucial point in the conference.

- If the school administrators tell you, "Of course we want your child. Here is what your child must do to get off of academic probation," then do what is required.

- If the administrators say they are not sure they want to keep your child unless your child can pull it together, then they probably will give your child another year at the school.

- If the school tells you, "No matter what, we do not want your child here next year," your course of action will be quite different.

After the meeting, make a plan. Do you have to find a new school, or was this notice the school's wake-up call to your child? Is this an offer to help? For some schools, this letter means your child either must attend summer school or he may not return in the Fall.

Some schools will automatically place a student who is on academic probation in the Spring quarter on the summer school list. This is important to know if you are making family plans for the summer. Unless your son or daughter attends summer school, they will not be invited back next year. Some schools will allow your child to take only the first three weeks of the summer class, if your child failed only the first semester of a class. It will count as the failed semester. An F for both semesters may require the full six weeks of summer class. This varies with schools.

Some schools will allow a class in the summer at another school. Check with your school administration <u>before</u> enrolling in the class you assume will be accepted. Some schools may accept private tutoring. Some offer a test sometime during the summer, usually late summer to demonstrate proficiency. Know and understand the school's policy regarding academic probation and returning for the next academic year. For example, one school sent a notice of academic probation and offered three semesters to raise the grades. This may be a time to consider an evaluation by an educational specialist or psychologist.

Academic probation notices can be a tremendous shock to the student and the family. An evaluation at this time will help your child know where best to put his energy. An evaluation will also determine if there are learning disabilities, learning delays, poor study skills or other problems. After you have a learning skills profile, then you and the professional can design a program that most effectively matches your child's learning style.

Grade Inflation

Grades have changed over the years. Twenty-five years ago a "C" meant average or on grade level. In many schools, a "C" now is unacceptable and most students receive "A's" and "B's." What would have been a "C" is now a "B". An "A" used to mean exceptional effort and performance. Today, an "A" means "very good," which is what a "B" used to be.

Some teachers start out by issuing lower grades, even though a child is doing outstanding work, under the guise of giving them room in which to grow. The problem with this plan is that it gives an inaccurate picture of the child's performance and an unrealistic expectation emerges. Parents may become critical or put unreasonable pressure on the child. If you have a question about whether a grade accurately reflects your child's performance, check with the teacher or review your school policy.

Parent Reaction

Parents and children race each other to the mailbox. Who gets to read the grades first? With a very young child, the parents should read the reports first, away from the child. It may or may not be appropriate to show him the report card, because a young child is not capable of the critical thinking required to interpret grades and evaluations. A summary from the parent will usually satisfy a child who is curious about his progress.

A parent's purpose in discussing grades is to develop a plan of action. Neither you nor your child should feel overwhelmed or helpless as a result of these reports. Overreaction by the parent can result in a child's going into denial, feeling fearful, rebelling or eventually completely shutting out the parent. To avoid reactions like these from your child, manage the discussion like a partnership, so your child sees that you and he are on the same team.

Use questions designed to gather information such as:

- "Did you have a chance to study for the math test that the report said you failed?"
- "Have you tried to talk to your teacher?"
- "How can we help you?"
- "What would you like us to do?"
- "What is your plan for approaching the situation?"

Questions and statements to avoid:

- "What's wrong with you?"
- "What's the matter, don't you understand what's happening?"
- "Have you been going to class?"
- "How could you have missing assignments?"
- "How could you have low test scores?"
- "Aren't you doing any of your work?"
- "Why can't you be more like your brother?"

- "Why didn't you try very hard?"
- "You are just like your relatives on your mother's side."
- "I asked you continually if you had homework and you said no."
- "You talk on the phone too much."
- "You play with your friends too much."
- "You don't take school seriously."
- "You'll never go to college at this rate."
- "You watch too much television."
- "All you care about are your electronic games."

Positive questions to ask include:

- "How do you feel about this grade?"
- "Is that a fair grade?"
- "Did you try your best?"
- "Does that grade reflect your efforts?"
- "Do you have a plan?"

<u>Good Grades</u>

How parents react to good report cards and good grades on tests and projects is also important, but parents first need to ask the child how he feels. Take your cues from his response and watch for a sense of pride or self-deprecation. It may be enough to say, "I am proud of your effort and I am proud of your doing the best job you could do." You might add, "I hope you feel very good about that." Keep in mind that the goal of grades is not the grade; it is designed to show whether your child has learned something about a topic or subject.

<u>Peer Competition, Pressure to Perform and Incentives</u>

Encourage your child to compete against himself to do quality work for his own pride of accomplishment. Julie was afraid to get A's because it would make her "stand out." She told her mom "You can't blend in with an 'A'."

For some children, praise or acknowledgment of their effort is enough reward for good grades or projects done well. They have their own internal motivation and their own internal reward system.

Some children are influenced by other children's rewards. One child said, "I want to be paid for my 'A's' because my friend Francine is paid for her 'A's'. She got $10 for each 'A', so I want $10, too." Even though the parents told her they did not believe in paying money for grades, they were open-minded. This was so important that they made an exception. This decision was controversial and we feel that the family philosophy needs to be discussed. Keep in mind what actually works for the child, *not what should work but does not work.*

There are children who regard money as an incentive for getting good grades. School is the child's job and sometimes, tangible rewards are necessary. Certain children will work harder for grades if they receive money for those grades. If you know that your child will work hard and to his best capacity with the learning as the reward in itself, do not jump in too quickly to add money for an incentive. Some children like material things as an incentive. Make the prize in proportion to the achievement.

One third-grade parent provided an incentive for her daughter to learn her multiplication tables by creating a replica of an Olympic Gold Medal. "This is for you when you have learned all your times tables." Another child in the class went home and explained to her mother what her friend's mother was doing and asked what she would get for mastering her times tables. Her mother replied she would get her heartiest congratulations. Both methods worked; it all depends on your family philosophy.

Some middle and high school students try to hide progress reports and report cards or even alter their grades. If this happens, have a calm discussion with your child. You might even want to give everybody a cooling-off period and schedule a time, even if it is only 45 minutes later, where you discuss the grades calmly.

Children's Reactions

Occasionally, children expect one grade and get another. Sometimes they are unrealistic about the effort they have put forth; at other times they have reason to be surprised and disappointed or feel the grade is an injustice. If your child blames the teacher, meet with the teacher and the child. The goal is to set an action plan for future grades.

Incentives

The number one incentive for improvement is encouragement. Without accusing your child, gather information from your child and/or the teacher. This is an opportunity to let your child know that you are working together and that you have a common goal to help him achieve his best at school. Children take on the most responsibility when they are part of the process and feel that you understand what they are experiencing. Being supportive and sympathetic will encourage your child to confide in you and will help him find ways to improve academic performance. Being sympathetic does not mean joining your child in excuses. Help your child feel that you are his ally.

Action Plans

Action plans may first require a full evaluation of your child's learning style. Gather information from the school about the class. Your child may not be the only child struggling. A teacher, who formerly taught third grade and is now teaching first grade, may not have sufficiently adjusted the curriculum downward and may need to make adjustments. Possibly your child may have a learning delay, a learning disability or an attention deficit, which has yet to be identified.

Time management may be a problem for your child. To improve that area:

- Teach time management techniques
- Organize time for study
- Learn test-taking strategies
- Obtain a tutor or an educational therapist
- Reorder priorities, or change extracurricular activities
- Modify the school schedule
- Designate a family study time

TESTS

Tests are given to measure competence. Standardized tests, which are designed to measure classroom performance across the nation, the effectiveness of teaching and individual child performance, have existed through most of this century. Standardized tests rarely measure for qualities such as creativity, tenacity, cooperation and determination.

Although imperfect, tests are also used as admission standards and to measure the culmination of a semester of work. Test makers continually try to reduce cultural bias in the tests, although this issue remains unresolved. Children with significant learning differences and English as-a-second-language students (ESL) continue to be put at a disadvantage on standardized tests. The main purpose of tests must be of competence, and should not hinder future success or cause a loss of self-confidence.

Testing Skills

Tests are an important part of a child's educational experience and serve as a valuable educational tool. A wide variety of tests are used throughout the year to measure students' progress and to determine which areas need bolstering.

Most states use standardized tests to compare a child's ability against standards and norms. A computer printout of these test scores is generally available to parents. Standardized test scores and test taking ability can be very important for future school placement. Many private schools lean heavily on these scores as criteria for entrance.

Knowing how to take tests is a crucial skill. Many schools give practice tests to prepare students, and these drills often distract from regular curriculum. On the other hand, tests are a reality in the lives of students, and practicing and learning to become "test smart" has benefits.

Find out your school's policy on practice tests and giving your child experience in the test setting. Some children do not do well in the first year of standardized testing. In the second year they have more knowledge and experience and because they have had practice taking tests, they do better.

Most standardized tests come in booklets. Children need to learn to work their way through the pages. Practice and visual familiarity with these booklets do improve test scores. It is like driving home from a new job: the first day it seems like a very long ride and you are not sure of your route; three weeks later you are on automatic pilot. Practice and familiarity are what some children need to reduce their anxiety and increase their speed and efficiency.

Preparing for a Test

Throughout your child's academic career, one constant is THE TEST. Spelling tests begin in early elementary school and become the focal point of the week. It is a way of evaluating memory not mastery of learning.

For good or ill, children make judgments about themselves based on early test performance. Skills need to be taught to students so that they can prepare for a test properly. Some children make flash cards and have the kind of memory that allows them to absorb the information off the flash cards. Other children need to make something that is called a mind map, which is like a tree with branches of all the different dynamics and aspects of the material. They need to literally see how the material intertwines and interrelates.

Try different strategies with your child. Sit with your child and figure out when the test will be given. Suppose your child tells you the test is on Friday. Say this is Monday. Ask your child if anything needs to be done about the spelling test on this day. Perhaps the answer is "no". Perhaps the answer is let's just look at the words to get a visual mind-set. The second step may be to actually write the words. The third step is to take a practice test. Work towards the Friday test with advance planning and practice.

Some teachers clearly identify the material that will be asked on a test. Other teachers, hoping that the student will study all aspects of the topic, are elusive about what will be tested. Students need to be organized in their study approach and systematic in preparing for all of the topics that will be included on the test.

Some students over prepare. Help your child learn the essential skill of differentiating what is important from what is not important. Ask your child:

♦ "What is important?"
♦ "What would you ask somebody after this chapter?"
♦ "What is important to know next week, next month, next year?"

Look through their study notes and study cards. Observe how well they outline the material. Can they pick out the salient points or prominent topics, or do they over focus on details? Balance is important.

Test-Taking Strategies and Test Anxiety

Obvious things such as being well rested, having a well-balanced meal and being as stress-free as possible, contribute to effective test taking. Stick to normal routines and operating rules at home. Talk about the test in advance. Reassure and encourage your child. At the same time, do not dwell on the subject, as this may cause anxiety. Let your child know that you understand that tests can be hard, but that taking them may provide a chance to show how well he or she can do.

Being comfortable is important. On the morning of the test, have your child get up early enough to avoid rushing. Be sure your child eats a good breakfast, but do not force a child to eat. Help him choose comfortable, familiar clothing and make sure he gets to school on time.

Many children who know the information find their anxiety blocks them from performing well on a test. Help your child focus on the test and away from their anxiety. One of the oldest techniques, and still one of the most useful, is to focus on breathing. Have your child take a slow deep breath as the test begins.

A technique that can be combined with breathing is visualization. Have your child picture himself working on that test and doing well. Another technique is to postpone writing anything for the first thirty to sixty seconds, and taking time to look over every question on the test. Have your child start with the ones he is most comfortable with.

Teach your child to pace his work. If your child is old enough and wears a watch, teach him to look at his watch and do something every ten minutes, such as wiggling his shoulders. Slowly rolling his neck or flexing his feet, pacing to redirect energy and maintain concentration, or looking up and away and then going back to work are other tricks that work.

Some children feel panicky when they look around and realize they are the last to finish a test. Reassure your child that he should take a test at his own pace so long as he finishes. The pace of other students means nothing as far as the score. Some children benefit from earplugs to filter out noise and distractions. Be sure your child wears glasses, if needed. Ask ahead of time if supplies are required.

We see students who get very involved in one question. Then, to their horror, they discover that there are two more to go and their time is up. For the older student who is wearing a watch, have him look at the time at the start of the test and look at the number of questions he must answer. Every once in a while he should glance back at the watch and see how much time is left.

Students with attention deficit disorders and other learning disabilities may request extended testing time. This request must be made many weeks before the exam. Proceed with caution in using this privilege, because there are schools and colleges that still look askance at a child who requires extended time or who needs a test to be administered individually. Weigh the benefits and disadvantages carefully.

Some standardized tests do not allow for a snack or rest room break. Your child should know this in advance in order to be prepared. Again, relaxing, deep breathing and stretching can refocus the mind. Remind your child to look up occasionally and rest his eyes. Teach him to think about focusing. If his mind wanders, he can silently rely on some personal cue words such as "focus", "now", and "attention" to alert himself to go back to his work.

Some tests require that the child attempt all answers with no penalty for wrong answers. On other tests, it is better to leave a question blank if he does not know the answer because points are subtracted for wrong answers. If this can be determined ahead of time, it will help prepare students for the best way to approach the test.

Usually, it is best not to make a random guess but to make an educated guess. For example, in a multiple choice question your child can usually eliminate one or two of the choices as being obviously wrong and then make the best choice between the two remaining answers.

Strategies for Test Preparation:

- Make a study plan and time frame, then follow it.
- Study when you are most alert.
- Review important material about two hours before going to sleep. (Recent research suggests that the memory system in the brain continues to consolidate learning while we sleep.)
- Take a practice test in a public place such as a library or cafeteria to simulate real testing conditions.
- Analyze errors on the practice tests, look for areas to reinforce.
- Use study buddies if they reinforce learning. Do not use them if they create more fear and anxiety.
- If you have memory problems, reinforce memory by practicing or use mnemonics (tricks to enhance memory).
- Remind yourself that examinations are a ticket, a passage to the next step.
- Visualize or rehearse test taking.

Fay counseled a boy who was highly anxious because his school was about to commence a full week of standardized testing. She provided a strategy to decrease his worry. She started out by asking him what the room would look like when the test started. He proceeded to describe how the desks were moved around, how he would walk into the classroom and that a booklet would be on each desk. This technique, which is often called mental rehearsal, made it possible for this boy to relax and concentrate on his test.

Once your child learns how to practice this technique, it can be useful on many levels. Sports teams use mental rehearsal, which reduces actual practice time and increases scoring. Break the scene down for your child, as much as you can, so that by the use of visualization, he can see in his mind what that testing room will look like. Encourage him to visualize himself calmly sitting there, taking slow deep breaths and doing fine.

Anticipatory anxiety causes some children to enlarge the whole testing experience, and the test then becomes a gigantic demon. Have your child visualize the test experience in a shrinking machine so that it is reduced to an eight and a half by eleven inch piece of paper—or even smaller. To help your child get through what may be an anxiety-producing situation, give him something to look forward to by planning something special after the event is over.

If your child has difficulty falling asleep before a big test, try something relaxing: a warm bath, a warm drink at bedtime or a cozy evening the night before the test. If the testing starts on Monday, have a family experience on Sunday evening to divert test anxiety. Some children relax and increase their confidence by using the mental rehearsal technique previously mentioned.

Give your child permission to not know everything on the test. Many children start to have anxiety reactions when they reach those problems they are not yet able to solve—and they shut down. The rest of the test then becomes a failure. Before the test, have your child tell himself there will be some things he knows, some things that he almost knows but can guess at, and some things that he has not learned yet. Focus on the word "yet." If he does not know it this year, he will know it next year.

The best part about taking a test is that at a certain point, it is over. However, many students cannot resist the urge to compare answers immediately after the test. This is a sure-fire way for them to get upset. Suggest another topic of conversation to have ready instead and encourage your child to just let it go. When someone asks your child how he did, suggest that he just say he did his best.

We also urge parents to avoid interrogating their children after a test. Instead ask: "How was the test today?" When you get the test results, remember that this is just one "snapshot" of how your child is doing in school. It is not fruitful to compare your child's performance with that of your friends' or neighbors' children. Discuss any questions you or your child may have about the test with his teacher.

Retaking Examinations

There are myriad reasons a child might get a low test-score: They did not know the material thoroughly, a family situation interfered with their ability to study properly, or the test was poorly constructed and did not measure the child's true knowledge. Some teachers will allow a child to retake a test. Do not be afraid to ask if there is an opportunity to retake a test. Your child may want to demonstrate his knowledge. He may want to explain why he was unable to demonstrate his knowledge before. For some students, the opportunity to retake a test brings a sense of closure and accomplishment.

The learning process includes understanding your teacher's style. Different teachers encourage different kinds of behavior. One approach is to ask if there is extra credit work for extra points. Some teachers are open to this, while others are not. One English teacher allows students to rewrite a paper until it reaches their satisfaction. The teacher continues to grade it and give comments until the student says, "All right, I'm satisfied. I'll take the B+ or the A- or whatever the grade is." It is up to the student to decide when he or she has reached the end.

Professional Resources

Test-taking strategies and study-skills classes are widely available from private companies and private tutors. These classes are usually designed for middle and upper school students. A good test-preparation class teaches the <u>how</u> of test taking. The emphasis is not on content but on strategies such as "psyching out" the test. Many students benefit from these programs, although these classes usually do not make dramatic differences in test scores. Even a small increase in scores can increase a child's confidence in approaching tests.

Ask for the credentials of the teachers and find out what curriculum will be taught in the test-taking class. Strategies for how to write a creative essay, how to proof read, how to approach multiple choice, matching, completion and true false questions are valuable tools. Encourage your child to do their very best.

These are just a few ideas to start. Be creative. If your child discovers his own test taking approach and it is successful, then encourage him to use it. Use your knowledge of your child and what is comforting to him to help him empower himself and make himself comfortable, not just from external ideas, but from his inner ability to encourage himself.

CHAPTER 5

PROBLEM SOLVING SKILLS

Chapter Highlights

Critical and Analytical Thinking Skills
Empowering Children to Become Problem Solvers
Evaluate the Information
Problem Solving and Conflict Resolution
Problem Solving in Action
Teaching Problem Solving Strategy
Problem Solving Rules
Common Ways Children Deny Responsibility for a Conflict
Validation of Feelings
Common Characteristics That Can Trigger Ineffective Problem Solving
Problem Solving with Children
Consequences

HOW TO DEVELOP PROBLEM SOLVING SKILLS

Suggesting Solutions
Misunderstandings with Teachers
It's Not Fair!
Cooperative Learning
Looking for Alternatives
Checklist for a Crisis at School
Problem Solving Worksheet

One of the most important skills for children to learn is how to get along with others. In this chapter, we will discuss various approaches to problem solving and outline techniques that can help you teach your children how to resolve conflicts to their satisfaction. People are not harmed by disagreement; however, they may be harmed by a lack of resolution.

Critical and Analytical Thinking Skills

Thinking through a situation from several angles and trying to understand it from another's viewpoint broadens our fund of information. In our childhood, we were told to STOP, LOOK and LISTEN before we crossed the street. This is the perfect metaphor for how to help children learn this skill. **STOP** telling children what to do. **LOOK** at your options. **LISTEN** to their answers.

People communicate more effectively when they use active listening tools. An active listener has the ability to self-monitor, by noticing the volume of his or her voice and body language. An active listener shows respect for another person's space and notices their body language. He or she also pays attention to and shows interest in that person's story, and reacts appropriately.

Empowering Children to Become Problem Solvers

The following open-ended questions lead to active listening. We suggest that you practice using them.

- How do you feel about what happened?
- What do you think would be another approach?
- When your friend made that choice, what was he thinking?
- How did you make your decision?
- If you had it to do over again, what would have been a better choice?
- What will you choose next time?

Many parents complain that it takes a great deal of time to have these discussions. That is true. But if we had to pick one area of parenting that fosters the most independence and gives children the greatest future opportunity, it would be give-and-take analytic discussions between parent and child.

Evaluate the Information

Questioning reliable sources is a good habit. A very young child can learn to evaluate information from the Internet, a newspaper, magazines, television, a friend and from you, the parent. Many parents teach their children that these are wonderful sources of information, but they also teach them how to question.

If a friend says that Miss Jones is leaving in June because she was fired, teach your child to ask, "Oh, how do you know this?" That is a wonderful question to ask from any source of information. For example, people are getting all kinds of guidelines on the Internet. Some of that information is reliable and some of it is on the level of grandma's superstitions. Some Internet information is helpful and some dangerous. Teach your child to ask in a calm manner, "How do you know this?" "Who told you?" "How did they hear about it?" In other words, what is the source of the information and is this a reliable source?

It is important to teach your child how to look at the reasons why information is being shared. They need to know that some people may have their special reasons for wanting pieces of information to be known, that some people claim to know things they actually do not know, and that some people say things which they know are untrue.

Problem Solving and Conflict Resolution

In both academic and social arenas, an effective student is an effective problem-solver. Here are some suggestions of ways to resolve problems when a conflict arises.

- Resolution to a dilemma can be reached by discussing a solution or an approach to the conflict.

- There are options if there is disagreement:

- If a discussion leads to no resolution of the dilemma, a decision to agree to disagree may be the best solution.

♦   A delayed decision or further discussion can occur if the nature of the problem is such that a solution or resolution must be reached, but cannot be resolved at the moment. There can be agreement to discuss it later, after each person has given more thought to the problem. Putting the interaction or discussion on hold for a later time serves as an interim solution.

♦   There are several ways to propose mediated compromises. One person freely acquiesces to the other person's viewpoint; the second person freely acquiesces to the first person; each freely acquiesces in part to the other person or to a totally independent option.

Problem Solving in Action

Anne Kessler, a teacher, who observed Brandi helping two boys resolve an altercation on the playground, describes the process this way:

"Brandi had the two children face each other and talk directly to each other. It was hard. They kept turning to her with accusations and denials, but she redirected them each time, until they finally got the hang of it. Brandi guided the interaction, making sure that each boy had the opportunity to express not only his perception of what had happened but also his feelings about it.

There had been a series of misunderstandings, which culminated in the incident. Once these misunderstandings were straightened out, there were apologies on both sides, forgiveness and a handshake. The boys walked back to their game arm in arm.

I asked Brandi if she could teach the other teachers and me how to do this magic. In twenty minutes, she outlined and demonstrated a simple procedure for dealing with conflict between students.

I certainly didn't expect the technique to work for me the way it did for Brandi. But incredibly, even though I didn't do it "right," it worked from my very first try. They talked to each other, they worked it out, they left satisfied—and it happened so quickly!

From then on, I felt like a teacher on the playground, not a cop or a judge. Yard supervision is now a pleasant part of my day, giving me energy rather than leaving me feeling tense and exhausted. And the benefits for the children are obvious. They are happier in the yard, return to their classrooms in much better shape emotionally, and they learn important skills about how to get along with each other."

Teaching Problem Solving Strategy

We can teach problem solving to adults and children in a very simple way. There are three stages to the strategy:

1 PAST	2 PRESENT	3 FUTURE
Dilemma: Tell what happened.	**Analysis:** How do you feel now? What are you thinking now? What are you doing now?	**Action:** What will you do next? (Accountability, apology, atonement and/or change of behavior)

Problem Solving Rules:

L A S T is the acronym for the problem solving rules:

- **Listen** actively
- **Accept** the undesirable 10%
- **Speak** only for yourself
- **Tell** the truth

L: Listening actively means you pay attention to all the communication signals (words, tone and body language) of the other person and yourself.

A: Accepting the undesirable 10% means that there is always a certain percent about a person that will not appeal to you. That percentage can fluctuate. The 10% can decrease to 5% or 2% making the person very tolerable. The behavior can increase to 20% making acceptance difficult but tolerated. There may be a person you will never understand, never like, or never fully accept. People often permanently end a relationship when the problematic situations reach 50%.

S: Speak only for yourself means that you avoid accusatory words such as "Why..." or "You...". Accusations cause people to become defensive. Beginning statements with words such as "What...", "When...", or "Could..." allow people to listen and respond with greater ease.

T: Telling the truth means that expressing honest and simple feelings or viewpoints is best. If people are clear in their communication, they will be believable and effective.

Common Ways Children Deny Responsibility for a Conflict

- He hit me first.
- He got in my way.
- He was too close to me.
- You don't like me anymore.
- You like him better.

Children make statements like these if they feel they do not have a voice in resolving the problem. They also say them to blame others. Responding to these defensive comments becomes a distraction from the situation at hand. The best plan is not to respond; simply say, "Regardless of whether or not that is true, this does not lead to a solution. Let's make a plan so you know how to handle a situation like this better next time."

Validation of Feelings

It is important to assure your child that you recognize that he feels strongly about what happened. Emphasize that it is your child's behavior you do not like, but that you like and love your child.

Common Characteristics That Can Trigger Ineffective Problem Solving

- Low level of tolerance
- Frustration
- Perfectionism
- Self-criticism
- Inability to inhibit behavior
- Immaturity
- Language delays
- Lack of training in problem solving
- Poorly modeled problem-solving behavior by parents

Problem Solving with Children

If your child is confused about a situation, give him an opportunity to process the information by talking with you and getting your feedback. If your child is unsure about what action to take, help him define the dilemma or the situation and have him tell you what he thinks would be the best solution. You empower your child when you encourage him to use his own resources, rather than having you provide the solution.

The six steps outlined below illustrate the sequence of problem solving:

1. For children to feel powerful, it is important that they know the problem-solving discussion will occur. At a calm time, ask your child to have a problem-solving session with you. Ask if he would like to discuss the problem immediately or think it over and discuss it in the future. The appointment for the problem-solving session should be set right then and adhered to. Be sure that you plan a specific time, but let your child select the time. They will be less likely to feel that there will be no resolution.

2. Refer to the problem as "a situation", "a dilemma" or "an issue to be solved." Avoid judgmental language such as "problem" or "a bad child."

3. Styles and approaches to processing information vary among individuals. Reassure your child that it is okay for the two of you to view the situation differently

There are goal-oriented people and there are process-oriented people. When there are options, process-oriented people like to think the situation over, process the information, reach their conclusion, and then discuss it. Goal-oriented people are more immediate, preferring to make a plan right away and implement the plan immediately. Misunderstandings occur when people get impatient with differing styles.

4.   Begin by asking your child if he has some thoughts about the situation. For example, the issue may involve hitting a sibling. Very often children want physical contact. They really want a kiss or a hug but they push or shove or pinch instead. Explain to your child about the difference between positive and negative touching.

5.   Ask your child for ideas to solve the dilemma. For example, ask your child to think of other ways to tell people what he wants, rather than hitting them.

6.   Listen to his viewpoint. Then ask your child what he thinks your opinion is about this, which is another way to give your child a chance to express himself. Do not over talk; be succinct.

As a parent, make an effort to answer your child's questions completely and clearly, not partially or with a fragment of a thought. Ask questions if you are unsure how to respond. Notice if your child continues to listen and appears to understand or if he is distracted or thinking of other things. Paraphrase or give feedback about what he said, so you can take the next action if requested or respond appropriately during the conversation.

If your child is having trouble identifying his feelings, offer several choices. For example, ask, "Max, do you feel angry or sad?" It helps to model feelings for your child by demonstrating and expressing emotions appropriately. Often, it is enough just to express happiness, sadness, anger, disappointment or fear.

If your child responds to a problem with a tantrum or by demanding his way, it will probably be ineffective to try to have a calm conversation at that time. Waiting for a child to calm down can take a few minutes, a few hours or a few days, but it is best to wait for a calm time, before asking your child to have a problem-solving session with you.

If the situation is volatile, have your child take a break. Some of the things you could say are, "Maybe you/we could use a break" or "You don't have to talk about it right now" or "When everyone is calm, we'll talk about it."

Consequences

Consequences are a natural outgrowth of behavior and situations as they arise. More and more, we are seeing children whose parents are over-protective and over-involved. By shielding children too much, we create a false sense of consequences. Sometimes, children are helped best when left to complete a project on their own. They may surprise everyone and succeed; they may flounder and ask for help or they may even fail, experiencing a natural consequence.

Consequences for a child's action must meet three conditions:

1. They must be meaningful and understandable to the child
2. They should be related to the wrongful act
3. The severity should be proportional to the misdeed

"Spare the rod and spoil the child" was a common ethic in earlier generations. Spanking in the home remains legal under American law unless it is physically harmful. Spanking is very memorable to children. They remember the feeling of fear or humiliation. Ask anyone who got "a belting," and they will tell you what it was for, but rarely do they report a way it helped. In fact, they frequently report further determination to get their own way. Punishment does not usually work. While punishment can inhibit behavior, it may not lead to a solution; neither may it lead to a permanent, general change in behavior. If it takes the responsibility for changing the behavior away from the child and puts it on the parent or enforcer, punishment is unlikely to provide a learning experience.

We strongly urge you not to use spanking as a method of disciplining your child, and do not permit your school to spank your child. It may be true that you feel that your child needs a spanking, but it will only reinforce the wrong message. Physical punishments harm your child. Hitting a child can quickly cross a line from a swat to an abusive hit; it greets violence with violence. "Don't hit your brother," WHACK! It is counterproductive to say "don't hit" and then hit your child.

Restitution in the form of time-outs and loss of privileges are far more effective. Time-outs are given when the situation is heading in a direction that neither parent nor child likes. A time-out can also become an exercise for calming and reflection. An appropriate statement might be: "Let's each take a moment to take a deep breath, step into separate corners and then come back and begin our resolution phase."

A time-out should be in direct proportion to the age of your child. A time-out of more than three minutes for a three-year-old is probably excessive and likely to negate learning. A ten-minute time-out for a ten-year-old may be appropriate.

Grounding does not always lead to positive actions; often it is just punitive. The child may be left with anger at the parents and no way to solve the problem the next time. Grounding also sends a message that it is a terrible thing to be home with your family. The child may say: "So what, you have grounded me. This doesn't hurt me. I'll play music and computer games."

Time-outs and grounding if you employ them must have built-in accountability plans. For example, when a child is sent to his room or into a corner to read or write down his feelings about what happened, the expectation might be for him to come back and say, "Next time I leave my lunch at home, I will not hit you. I will not demand more food!" I'll say "Could we please stop and get lunch because I'm hungry." The other value of a time-out is that it creates a cooling off period for the people in a volatile situation.

It helps to think in terms of "response cost," which means that a child has a consequence for his action and a way to make amends for the problem he created. For example, if he stole money, he must replace the money. If he hurt someone, he has to spend extra time playing with that child. Making amends is more than a million apologies; it means giving back, either to the person who was hurt or to someone else, as a way of paying for the hurt that was caused.

If parents are separated, the punishment usually should not carry over to the other parent's house unless both parents are already involved in the situation. Sometimes the uninvolved parent needs to be notified but not drawn into the situation.

HOW TO DEVELOP PROBLEM SOLVING SKILLS:

1. _Allow children to fail or succeed on their own._ As parents, it is natural to want your child to succeed; ironically, success often depends on early failure. When we encourage our children to view a "failure" as an opportunity to learn an approach or

gain information, we give them a powerful key to success. If a child is devastated because he did not get the wonderful grade or comments he was looking for, rather than saying, "Oh that miserable teacher didn't appreciate all the hard work you did" try saying, "Let's take a look at this. It may be hard for you to look at it but let's see what we can learn from this."

2. *Revisit the situation at a later time.* "If you had this to do again, now that you have more information, what would you do?" This crucial question leads your child to learn from failure. By asking about "the next time," you help your child look to the future rather than dwelling on a past failure. This technique helps your child transforms failure into useful information.

3. *Teach survival skills.* The child who learns to analyze and solve problems has a greater chance of survival in the outside world than the child who merely memorizes facts. In our fast paced technological society, facts quickly become obsolete. Teaching your child to analyze situations and develop possible solutions gives him critical skills he will need in today's world. The following are some essential survival strategies to teach your child:

- When and how to walk away from a negative situation.
- How to set up a buddy system for walking across campus, through the park, or returning home.
- How to control fears and maintain a balance of caution.
- When to have eye contact and when to avoid it.

The most effective self-defense classes maintain that the number one defense is knowing when to get out of a potentially dangerous situation. They teach strategies and ways to yell as well as how to use defense tactics. The challenge for parents is convincing our children and ourselves that even with self-defense classes, we can be vulnerable and we must be cautious, yet not live in fear.

When bad things happen, remember to apply the 5-to-1 rule: One large negative needs five positive experiences or messages to counteract it. For example, if you see an attack (negative), then review five positives:

1. Who came to assist?
2. Who followed up?

3. Who provided care?
4. Who provided treatment?
5. What was done to avoid a repetition of the problem?

Suggesting Solutions

Sometimes a parent can suggest a solution if the child is blocked on the problem-solving task. A parent could say: "You may not have physical contact with another person to solve the problem." Here are some other choices for you to release your feelings or to make your feelings known to the other person or get what you want:

- Draw a mad picture
- Designate a pillow for pounding, and pound it
- Write a letter
- Speak to a tape recorder
- Hit a punching bag
- Talk to the person directly or on the phone
- Run around the block
- Count to 10 before you speak or act
- Jump on a trampoline
- Exercise, play basketball, etc.
- Take a bath

Misunderstandings with Teachers

School projects or examinations often stir up feelings of injustice. School projects demand a combination of abilities including organization, academic aptitudes and critical thinking skills. The most effective teachers write down the criteria for a project and then monitor their students' progress along the way.

Teachers need to consider extraneous circumstances and situations beyond the control of the student or his family. Common examples are students who cannot organize or plan a long-term project due to a possible learning difference, or students who experience an unexpected event, such as a visitor, a death, a trauma or an illness.

In our experience, most teachers attempt to accommodate individual needs. However, we know of situations where the opposite was true, and unfortunately, not all unfair situations have a recourse. One student's home computer failed in the middle of a term project. Her mother spent $60 at a photocopy and computer store so her child could complete the assignment on time. In spite of the family's extra effort, expense and inconvenience, the teacher graded the student down because one page was handwritten. This seemed unfair.

Another student, new to a school, had never written a report before. The teacher made no allowances for this fact, either in her comments or in her grading. This also seemed unfair. These are examples of teachers without compassion.

Some children can take disadvantages like these in stride, while others are less able to manage injustices in life; still others ruminate about an injustice and even think of revenge. Ideally a child will look at what happened, consider the source, and evaluate options. For example, they might ask themselves, "Should I talk to the teacher?" or "Should my parents intervene?" "Should I chalk it up to experience?" Better yet, "Should I treat the situation as information or a lesson, a chance to be flexible or as a simple injustice which I cannot change?"

Typically, the same project will be required of all students who are in the same grade level but in different classrooms. One teacher may interpret the assignment one way, while a teacher in another classroom may present it differently. The idiosyncrasies of each teacher may enter into the grading criteria for the project. If a teacher is detail oriented, he may require pictures or fancy artwork. If a teacher is content oriented, she may expect carefully written work and not value drawings as much.

Ideally, all grading standards would be the same. However, some schoolwork has to be done to "please the teacher" because he is the one issuing the grade. If the child will not recognize and accommodate to the requirements set by the teacher, then the student may be disappointed by his grade.

As a parent, try to remain objective about the situation. Help your child appraise the situation and help him determine the best solution. Avoid taking your own action to rescue your child. Use your problem-solving skills:

- Discuss what happened
- Consider the situation an experience and decide to take no action
- Formulate an effective plan

Action plans might incorporate some of the following steps:

- Politely present the situation to the teacher, who may be unaware of certain facts. Be respectful, because there may be more about the situation than you are aware of.

- Let go of the whole thing. Accept what happened.

- Call for an appointment with the teacher or arrange for a telephone conference. Be sure your child is included in the meeting or telephone call. If not, you may be caught in a triangle of "she said, he said."

- Explain the circumstance that you feel the teacher did not know about or did not understand clearly.

- Ask for something specific such as a changed grade, an added comment page considering the new information, or a chance to change what was graded down, either by redoing the work or amending it.

- Last resort: Meet with the counselor or principal to discuss the situation and your concerns. Be specific about how you expect them to intervene.

It's Not Fair!

Life is filled with incidents and outcomes that are not fair. Each of us must tolerate inconsiderate behavior at the hands of others who think and view the world differently from us. Students must endure the occasional teacher who makes unreasonable demands.

To teach your child how to accept and/or deal with difficult situations, it is crucial that you LISTEN to your child's expectations and disappointments. Parents often fall into traps that make a child feel as if he were not listened to: For example saying "You do not need to be upset about that" denies or disrespects a genuine feeling.

Parents do not have to agree with their child's position, but it is important to recognize that you know when your child has a different viewpoint. Telling your child, "I know you are disappointed. What would you like to do now?" or "What action plan do you have in mind?" will help him feel he has a voice about the situation.

Unfairness exists in real life. Disappointments exist. The opportunity to evaluate a disappointment is an opportunity for a child to grow in self-confidence and to define himself. Not being selected for a tennis team can bring a variety of responses. Some quit, saying "I hate tennis and I do not want to play." Others become motivated and say, "You will have me on it next year."

Cooperative Learning

The popularity of cooperative learning approaches in schools has increased. Therefore, it is likely that there will be times in every student's career when he will be faced with group projects or cooperative learning.

In general, two or more students are expected to work together to complete a project or paper. Each person receives the same grade or credit for the collective effort. This method of teaching can produce either positive or negative results.

For example, a group of incoming seventh graders received a group project. One girl, Jane, assertively took the lead. She ordered the group members around saying, "You do this, you do that." She came across as so smart and controlling that the group deferred to her.

In fact, Jane could not really organize the project. The group let her control them. Later they were sorry when they got a "C". Some of the girls felt angry. These girls did not know who would be the best leader. They did not recognize that Jane was all bravado until it was too late. On the next project, they will do one of several things: ostracize Jane, dominate her, redirect her or let her lead again. Help your child to learn from these kinds of experiences, and guard yourself from being too harsh on Jane. She needs guidance too.

It is not uncommon for one child to expend more effort than others in the group are. By making the projects either pass/fail or not graded, a teacher can remove the competitive aspect and leave room for cooperation. Children can be taught how to work as a team and to implement strategies to organize the project, to divide the labor fairly and to monitor progress leading to the conclusion. Opportunities to discuss the process afterward will add meaning to dissecting how well the experience has progressed. A summary sheet at the end of each report, asking for each child's personal experience, will allow the teacher to hear various expressions of how the project went.

Looking for Alternatives

Dilemmas, which require problem solving and critical thinking, occur daily. Consider a typical dilemma 12-year-old Travis had to face.

It was election time. For homework, the teacher told students to cast his or her vote on a copy of a ballot, putting their name at the top of the paper. The parent was required to sign the ballot. One proposition was particularly controversial. It involved the school's future and that of the minority children at that school. The pressure and problems were obvious to all. Travis was afraid to vote his conscience because his teacher was going to see his ballot. Instead, he voted the way he thought she would want him to.

Many alternatives existed for Travis and his parents that would have saved this assignment from catastrophe.

- Asking Travis how he wants to vote
- Accepting his choice
- Taking the opportunity to analyze the proposition and all its pros and cons so he can practice how decisions are thought through and made after consideration of all sides
- Photocopying the ballot and voting one way in secret (the way it is in real life); then voting the "politically correct" way and turning that in to the teacher with a note explaining how it was decided

Checklist for a Crisis at School

1. Information gathering—Gather as much information from your child as you can. For example, if he is avoiding school, ask him what part of the school day he likes best? What part of the school day does he wish would never happen again?

2. <u>Gather information from other sources</u>—Get information from other parents and other children, if it can be done in an unobtrusive manner. Visit the class to see for yourself. Is the teacher sarcastic? Is something frightening or unsettling to your child? If you sense it also, then validate your child's feelings as you begin to make a plan of action.

3. <u>The teacher step</u>—Bring information in a written format to school. Take your child with you to the meeting with the teacher. Enlist the teacher's help in making this situation better. Orient the meeting toward problem solving, not accusation. Otherwise, the teacher or the other child is likely to defend the conduct rather than solve the problem.

4. <u>Involve an administrator if necessary</u>—If there is no satisfactory resolution, consult with the administration or your child's counselor. Let her help guide you to a solution. If you think this might become a difficult situation with a teacher whom you perceive to be uncooperative, include the administrator in the teacher meeting at an early stage.

5. <u>Follow-up</u>—Monitor the situation every three days, at first, then once a week, then every two to three weeks.

PROBLEM SOLVING WORKSHEET

Write down a problem and the plan to solve it. When tempers are so hot or feelings are so hurt that talking will not lead to a conclusion, writing can help. This is an especially helpful technique for people who are visual learners or whose verbal skills are limited.

1. Describe the problem you want to solve:

_____
_____
_____
_____
_____

2. How do you feel about what happened? Describe your reaction and emotions.

_____
_____
_____
_____
_____

3. What are the differing viewpoints of what happened?

I see it this way:

_____
_____
_____
_____
_____

I propose the following resolution:

_____
_____
_____
_____
_____

You see it this way:

_____
_____
_____
_____
_____

You propose the following resolution:

_____
_____
_____
_____
_____

4. Decision or solution:

Agreement reached:_____

Agreement to disagree:_____

Delayed decision:_____

Compromise:_____

NOTES:

CHAPTER 6

LEARNING STYLES AND LEARNING DIFFERENCES

Chapter Highlights

A commonly held misconception is that a typical classroom has a homogeneous group of students. Children, however, vary widely in their attributes and talents. They also differ in their learning styles. In this chapter we will address various factors that affect learning, including intelligence, rates of learning and processing speed, and emotional development. Because children tend to use their abilities according to their individual learning style, we will discuss ways to identify your child's learning differences.

What Is Learning?

Learning differences need to be identified early. Plan and implement an intervention to remediate those deficits which can be remedied and/or teach compensatory skills. With remediation or compensation the child can learn in the best way possible.

For our purposes, we define learning as a change in behavior that occurs as a result of experience. Learning is also about opening up to something new or taking a risk to view something with a new vision and a new way of thinking. At times this process may be uncomfortable, mundane or unfamiliar, and a child may resist.

Processing speed is an important aspect of the ability to learn. Processing speed is the time it takes a child to complete a task. Information that is processed is both absorbed and utilized. How well a child focuses, processes in depth, and understands details affects his ability to use the learning. Some children are reflective learners, they move more slowly through new learning material than others. A reflective child could be misdiagnosed as a child with an attention deficit disorder. The reflective child may have some attentional issues but the predominant feature is the slower processing speed. The reflective child takes extra time to answer questions and may not score as well on timed tests. This child frequently needs an opportunity to take tests on an extended time basis.

Persistence at a task is a cornerstone of learning. Because it is not always innate, persistence needs to be taught. Teaching children how to focus and remain attentive is important, especially when it comes to the critical issue of remembering information.

What Is Intelligence?

Intelligence has many facets, including the ability to acquire information, word knowledge, motor and processing speed, comprehension, and critical and analytic thinking skills. Intelligence also includes creativity, musical ability, writing talents and social skills. Some of these abilities are measurable on standardized tests and some are not.

In general, intelligence is the ability to accumulate new knowledge, to remember previous learning and to reason. Intelligence is how a person processes, retains, analyzes and retrieves information. When we test for intelligence, we test for retention of knowledge accumulated from prior learning. We ask people to attempt tasks that test their aptitude for learning new material or to apply skills to unfamiliar material. We measure a person's verbal ability, perceptual acuity, and the capacity to function on timed or speed tests.

What Are Learning Styles?

Because people process information through different neuro-developmental channels, a classroom must accommodate various learning styles. Human brains vary in their abilities. Learning styles are how each of us approaches learning. Mel Levine, M.D. discusses all kinds of minds in his research on neuro-developmental differences. The ability to learn and apply skills is a complex process between multiple brain functions.

Learning is an interweaving of abilities including memory, language, attention, perception, motor development, higher order cognition, critical thinking skills, sequencing and spatial ordering. Environmental, cultural, temperamental, emotional and social factors also influence educational progress.

Children learn best when they identify their own learning strengths and weaknesses and when they understand that variation in ability is normal. When parents understand the development of different learning areas and the increasing complexity of demands on learning, they become more able to help their child have success in school.

Although there are many individual learning styles, three of the main pathways to learning are auditory, visual and kinesthetic. A quick way to determine if you are an auditory, visual or kinesthetic learner is to notice whether you make notes to enhance remembering things, just store information in memory after hearing it, or touch things and participate actively rather than merely watching or listening.

Auditory learners want to hear it. You can help your auditory learner focus by teaching him to listen to pauses and inflections in his teacher's speech. Teach him to go on "auditory alert" when he hears phrases such as "the first", "the reason why...", "in conclusion...", etc.

Visual learners grow impatient and feel overloaded without visual aides or cues to assist them. They may also create their own visual aids, such as outlines or drawings, as they absorb ideas. Help your visual learner focus in class by teaching him to read his teacher's body language clues. Most teachers shift their position or move to another part of the room when they change topics or before they make important announcements.

Kinesthetic learners need to learn by doing and by imitation. Kinesthetic learning is the primary system used by infants and young children; they learn with their bodies. Athletes are an example of this style of adaptation. They see something happen and they imitate it. Kinesthetic learners might express their learning style in the words of an old Chinese proverb: "I hear and I forget; I see and I remember; I do and I understand." The kinesthetic learner can help himself by writing notes or handling a physical object, such as a book. Using a highlighter, when permitted also helps the kinesthetic learner. Some children have difficulty utilizing kinesthetic feedback. The complex motor action of writing is a common source of difficulty in school. This becomes more pronounced when writing paragraphs enter the curriculum. Using accommodating devices such as a special pencil, pen or pencil grip that is comfortable for the hand is often helpful. Sometimes changing the pencil pressure is useful. Promptly addressing graphomotor (writing) delays is very significant for school success.

Collaboration between the parents and the school personnel is essential for maintaining a focus on a child's learning differences. It is essential to monitor your child's progress, watch for learning delays and understand how to provide the best intervention for your child's learning difference. Assess changing individual needs as your child progresses through the school years.

It is a challenge for schools to accommodate different individual needs as well as making distinctions between a learning difference and a learning disability. Beware of the label. Educators and other professionals are currently misusing many of the educational terms we will discuss. Often, children are misunderstood or misdiagnosed in the classroom. For example, children who are sensitive to noise may have greater difficulty with a teacher who has a loud voice or during noisy construction at the school site

Some children are labeled as behavior problems or uncooperative when, in fact, they may have an undiagnosed learning difference or learning delay. How does a parent figure it out? Pay close attention to when the behavior happens. Did it happen the year before with a different teacher or after a change in the home life? Does it occur only during reading time? If we misinterpret a child, the result can lead to behavior problems, under-achievement and low self-esteem. A mother told us:

"I never understood how important it was to know about learning styles. Now I realize from what you have taught me that most of our family is very verbal (auditory). But we have one daughter who is mostly a visual learner. In fact, when I ask her to do things, she frequently looks at me and says, 'Blah, Blah, Blah, Blah.' I now realize that she is letting me know in 15 seconds that she has an auditory overload. In her mind, the spoken words were a blur. She doesn't know how to communicate that to me. I want to thank you because now I am going home to let her know that I will begin to write things for her or I will begin to ask for feedback to be sure she understands what I say."

The integration of all the styles promotes the best understanding and learning. Helping your child to use all learning modalities will boost her school success.

It is important for teachers to recognize their own learning style. Traditionally, the classroom teacher has presented material in an auditory manner. Teachers with a strong auditory orientation will gravitate to this method. However, without a visual chart for students to look at in combination with a verbal presentation, the predominantly visual learner might miss important information.

Students remember what they have been taught if they are an active part of the educational process. This knowledge has led to the organization of more classrooms into what is called multi-sensory or multi-modal teaching. Materials and learning are presented with the opportunity for students to work cooperatively on projects. They can participate with the teacher on projects. When information is presented in both an auditory and visual manner, and with active student involvement, more processing is involved and greater learning takes place.

Summary: Every child has their own unique template for how they learn best. Happiness and academic success at school depend on a child feeling that they know what is expected and how to succeed competently. The different styles of learning interact at all levels of development, but with increasing complexity and with increasing demands in later years. Review your child's learning progress at all ages and stages. Help your child understand their strength and the areas that need strengthening. Have conversations about how they assess progress with their studies. Understand that a child's complete ability both to acquire skills and to demonstrate ability is a phenomenal interweaving of brain abilities. Identify learning differences. Remediate where possible and develop compensatory strategies for the rest.

How Can Parents or Teachers Intervene with Different Learning Styles?

It is helpful to discuss different approaches to learning and studying with your child. You might suggest these options:

- Write what you need to learn
- Tape record what you need to learn
- Draw what you need to learn

If your child is highly visual, learn to use visual language:

- Do you see what I mean?
- Do you see what I am trying to tell you?
- Do you have a picture in your mind of how you would do it differently next time?

If your child is primarily auditory, learn to use auditory language:

◆ Does this ring a bell?
◆ How does that sound?
◆ What do you think when you hear...?

Now That I Know About My Child's Learning Style, What Do I Do?

Once you have identified what learning style your child uses, you can be more effective in helping him study. If you discover that your child is an auditory learner and, for example, you are helping him study for a spelling test, have him say the word aloud, sound out the syllables and say each letter in the word. If you are teaching spelling to a visual learner, you will have him visualize the word to see it when he closes his eyes. Sometimes people who are very visual close their eyes before they answer when given a spelling test. For the kinesthetic child, encourage him to write or trace the word, in the air or on paper.

Memorizing words in isolation generally translates to very little long-term learning. It just becomes a memory exercise. The integrated learning of spelling comes when a word is written in the context of a sentence or a story. What do you do if your child is an auditory learner but has a teacher who uses a kinesthetic approach to spelling, where students must write three sentences using the word? Tell your child to say the word out loud as he writes it. You have now built in that extra dimension that you know works for your child. There are few children who are helped by writing the same word ten times. The majority of children see it as a futile exercise in handwriting and they usually resent it.

Some students become afraid to use their innate style because, in some school settings, children are taught to please their teacher. Having learned that grades are important, they direct all their efforts toward pleasing the teacher and meeting the requirements in order to get a good grade. As a parent, show appreciation to any teacher who recognizes the value of creativity and individuality by providing assignments that encourage their development.

Background Noise

Some students need quiet while learning and are distracted by even the mildest background noise. Earplugs provide a simple solution for some children who are noise-sensitive. Since various types are available, it is a good idea to have your child try out several to find the one that is most comfortable.

For other children, noise, particularly white noise, improves their learning. Reactions to white noise are highly individual. For a few students, television becomes white noise, which calms them down and allows them to study. For most others, all their attention will go to the television. Watch your child to see what works.

There are certain radio stations that some of our students have told us are effective white noise. In particular, these are stations that specialize in instrumental New Age music, which can be used as background music. Some people enjoy listening to classical music while they study. For creative writing, some students have found waltzes to be the preferred background music. Lyrics are rarely helpful as background music.

For a particular assignment, they may want to have a certain kind of background noise to set the mood. To associate specific music with work can become a strong stimulus for study and may help your child ease into the student mode. However, if your child is dancing and jumping on the bed, try something else and save the music for break time. One mother plays drums while her daughter dances; afterward her daughter studies.

Remain flexible. Allow your child to work in a variety of environments. For example, some children prefer the kitchen table to a desk in their room. Certain assignments may be done privately in a quiet place, while others can be done in the midst of people. It may depend on the subject or assignment.

The child who requires absolute quiet may benefit from the use of earplugs. You may want to set up a carrel (or privacy board), a three-sided cardboard enclosure that may be placed on a desk or kitchen table. In a sense you create a cubicle around a student.

Study Time and Study Breaks

The optimal study time, which can vary with a child's attention span, is usually twenty to thirty minutes. For a younger child it will be closer to twenty minutes. Study breaks are important but they should be short. We recommend twenty minutes on, five minutes off or thirty minutes on, ten minutes off. The child who cannot adhere to the five minutes may want to set a timer.

Research has demonstrated that studying is more effective and retention increases by having breaks. Many people associate a break with eating something; however, you do not want to make that the sole activity of any break. It could be a stretch, a walk around the house, moments to play with a sibling, shoot baskets or talk with a parent. It does mean moving away from where you have been working. The number one criterion of an effective break is, do not stay where you are.

Invisible Children

The invisible child is one who might fall through the cracks. They feel or are taught, "No one is supposed to notice us." When someone then does notice, these children are surprised and often act shy and introverted.

For example, the family of a high school student with learning disabilities thought he could blend in by keeping his learning disabilities a secret. The child kept the secret also, thinking he could make himself invisible. This resulted in disaster for the student; three months into the semester, he was failing half of his classes.

The lesson is to give your child the courage to go to his teachers and say: "I am capable of learning, but I have some learning delays and here's how they affect my work. If you would like more information about how I learn, here is my psychologist's name and number, or my tutor's name and number. They can explain how I learn best."

The Camouflaged Child

These children may look as if they are achieving on a much higher level than they are. There is often a "cottage industry" in place to keep the camouflaged child afloat in the classroom. This child experiences two schools: one where he or she is officially enrolled, and one at home. The school never sees how the child is really functioning because the parents and tutors are assisting too much.

Quiet, sweet children can also be camouflaged and sometimes fall through the cracks. As a parent, it is important to encourage them to be noticed and understood.

Attention Deficit Disorders (ADD)

Currently, one of the biggest topics in education is Attention Deficit Disorders (ADD). Attention deficits come in several forms:

- The inability to pay consistent attention and concentrate
- Impulsive behavior
- Hyperactivity
- Social and emotional problems such as oppositional behavior or conduct disorder problems

We need to make a distinction between Attention Deficit Disorders and Attention Deficit Hyperactivity Disorder or ADHD. Attention and concentration problems fall under the categories of ADD. Problems with hyperactivity and impulsive behavior tend to fall under the category of ADHD.

People often confuse forms of attention deficits with freedom from distractibility, which is the ability to concentrate, attend to a task and focus without being internally or externally distracted. Very often children are referred to psychologists for an evaluation of an attention deficit when either the classroom is not the correct environment for the child or the child cannot flourish there without medication. Psychotherapy and medication combined may be an excellent solution for that child. Educational therapy may be a necessary adjunct.

Attentional problems are rarely found to be isolated learning problems in and of themselves. They need careful evaluation. The ability to sustain attention, produce schoolwork, and follow through requires attention, memory, language ability, writing ability, organization and/or study skills.

There is also another kind of child who appears to have attention deficits, but his behavior may be an indication of boredom, or that the particular school or class may not be appropriate for that child. Another educational setting might so positively affect the child's behavior that medication may no longer be necessary. In some instances medication improves the quality of a student's life and in other cases medication is over prescribed.

Processing Speed

The fact that a child is reflective and progresses slowly with schoolwork needs to be evaluated carefully. It does not automatically mean that these students learn less than students who respond quickly; in fact, they may make fewer errors. Reflective students are often perfectionists in their work. They want to feel absolutely sure of themselves before they move forward. Reflective learners tend to ask parents, teachers and evaluators lots of questions. They also come back later and ask, "Was the answer to a certain question such and such...? or "Did I answer that part correctly?"

To distinguish between processing speed, distractibility and attention problems, you need to ask: "How does my child listen to directions and follow them?" If your child listens intently and then follows through, he is most likely a cautious, reflective learner. Children with processing speed problems can also have visual perceptual problems, hand eye coordination problems, or difficulty with paper and pencil speed. These students may need a thorough developmental optometry evaluation.

If your child is impulsive, works quickly, makes lots of errors and does not self reflect, he may be more of a distractible, inattentive or impulsive person. Pay attention to whether your child has difficulty with timed tests. To perform best they may need to take tests that are not timed.

Rates of Learning

Rates of learning can also be seen in the changing tempo of a child's learning. We call them Fall and Spring children. Some children, who take off in the Fall and work diligently and hard, often burn out by Spring. Other students take a while to figure out the teacher's demands and expectations. They wait to respond until they feel comfortable and proceed cautiously, but leap into action in Spring. Some children are steady and work the whole year diligently.

We see children who start kindergarten not knowing how to hold a pencil. Others enter kindergarten reading the alphabet. This is not a prediction of their future ability per se; it merely means they may have different life experiences and they may be processing at different learning rates.

The challenge of teaching is not to let anyone fall through the cracks simply because their learning rate is different. This raises complex issues of graded and non-graded classrooms and whether children should be compared to their peers on standardized tests if their rate of learning is different.

How Do Emotional Factors Affect Learning?

Learning is intertwined with temperament. So are learning disabilities, learning delays, attention deficits and hyperactivity. All of these are characteristics that may affect learning. They can be attributes or hinderances needing assessment. Part of your role as a parent is help your child use these characteristics to their advantage.

Temperament

Temperament leads to a unique behavioral style. We are less judgmental about children when we look at their behavior in terms of temperament. A combination of many factors including learning style, environment, genetics and the circumstances of the child's life can affect behavior.

There are many temperament traits but the research by Dr. Stella Chess seems to be the clearest. Her research identifies nine temperamental traits.

◆ Sensitivity—What is the sensitivity level of your child? Is your child highly sensitive or able to take things in stride? This includes physical as well as emotional sensitivity. (For example, how do his clothes feel, allergies, sun sensitivity.)

◆ Intensity of Reaction—This is the energy level of response. Your child's response may range from a tantrum to a low intensity shrug. Some children are intense in their reactions and may be misunderstood and labeled as angry or impulsive.

◆ Activity Level—Activity level can be high or low. Some children watch TV and jump around; some remain still and need silence.

◆   Adaptability—Adaptability is the response to change. Some children are flexible, while some are rigid. Some are slow to adapt to routines and some adapt quickly.

◆   Approach-Avoidance—Some children jump right into activities, while others hold back, stare, get their bearings and then participate. Still others hang back until they are completely comfortable.

◆   Persistence—Persistence is the ability to keep at a task until it is finished. Some children will stay with a task until you pull them away and some will flit from task to task.

◆   Rhythms—Rhythm refers to the regularity of the person. Examples include the regularity of the sleep-wake cycle or the prediction of bowels. Did your child in the first three months develop a style or were they irregular or chaotic?

◆   Quality of Mood—At different times a child can be friendly, fussy, joyful, or in pain. Some children seem generally unhappy while others seem perennially happy. Some children have difficulty in certain situations and not in others. Know your child's and your own moods as much as you can. Tailor activities accordingly. Know when to leave and when to stay. Many parents over-stay a visit and then wonder why their child is fussing.

◆   Distractibility—Length of attention span can vary with each child. Some children can be distracted and still on task and learning. Some children can be very persistent and others inconsistent or distractible.

NOTES:

CHAPTER 7

GETTING THE RIGHT
HELP FOR YOUR CHILD

Chapter Highlights

GETTING THE RIGHT HELP
   Learning Specialist
   Learning Disability – Learning Delay
   Learning Differences
   Evaluation
   When to Refer a Child for Help
   Home Schooling
   School Placement Specialists
   Other Approaches to Diagnoses and Treatment Plans

SPECIAL EDUCATION STUDENTS IN REGULAR CLASSROOMS
   Assisting Children With Special Needs
   Special Purpose Schools

OTHER RESOURCES AVAILABLE FOR CONSULTATION
   Psychotherapy
   Speech and Language Therapy
   Preparing for Entrance Exams
   Alternative Therapies and Treatment Opportunities
   Medical
   Mentors
   Caretakers
   Other Resources

When you are the parent of a special-needs child, you carry the burden of educating others as well as confronting your own feelings. This chapter is designed to help you select the correct services and/or the appropriate professionals to work with your child.

GETTING THE RIGHT HELP

Learning Specialist

If you decide to consult with a learning specialist, it is best to look for someone with a solid background in and an understanding of education and schools. Although the person you select does not necessarily have to be an educator, we recommend that you seek out someone with combined expertise in psychology and education and with special education training.

We offer these suggestions when you consult with professionals about your child:

♦ Interview several candidates and ask about their background and training in evaluating children and their learning needs. Are they familiar with advocating for children and knowledgeable about school placement?

♦ Explain your child's situation and ask how they would help.

♦ Will they collect an educational history and conduct an interview with your child's teachers so that information about the child's performance at school is complete?

♦ Ask if they plan to gather a behavioral history of your child.

♦ Valuable information can be derived from the following sources: a school observation, a meeting with both parents to get their views along with a detailed developmental history, a meeting with the caretakers who are involved with the child. Even siblings can offer input.

Learning Disability - Learning Delay

Parents frequently ask us how to tell if their child has a learning disability or a learning delay. What exactly is the difference? How do I know when my child should be referred for an evaluation? Can my child learn a compensatory strategy for learning problems, which are resolved by time alone?

Current research and understanding of learning ability is moving at a rapid pace. Experts such as Mel Levine, M.D. have written excellent materials for parents, teachers and students about learning differences.

A learning delay assumes that learning will take place later and will occur pretty much on its own with maturity. Learning differences tend to be life-long. Learning styles can be neurological and/or psychological in nature.

Analogy: A learning delay can be likened to the car that travels from Los Angeles to San Francisco. It may not get to San Francisco in seven hours but it will get there in ten. A learning difference, however, means that you will have to steer differently because the steering does not work the way it does on other cars. You will have to make true compensations for driving that car and acquire a different manuel on how to drive and maintain the car.

Learning Differences

A learning difference can make a student sensitive to certain kinds of teaching styles and certain types of curriculum. A learning difference is not a learning disability, but it does mean that a student is strongly locked in to a particular way of receiving information. In fact, she is so locked in, that other methods are not nearly as effective for this kind of student. When you have a child who is sensitive to a learning style and has a learning difference, battles over how to teach a subject can arise with teachers as well as with parents who try to teach their children.

One of the best ways to help a child is by matching her particular learning style with an appropriate teaching style. This is especially true in early elementary school where one teacher primarily controls the environment. If there is a dramatic difference between the teaching style and the student's learning style, changing teachers can bring about a substantial improvement.

When a child spends six hours a day with a teacher who does not teach in a way in which he or she can effectively learn, this does not necessarily indicate the child has a learning disability. We recall a teacher who had an ongoing conflict with a child with very high intelligence. The child, who had been flourishing in a previous classroom, was no longer doing well. To have a conflicted, disrupted school year due to the extreme differences in teacher and student style was going to harm her psychologically as well as educationally. In this case, we recommended making a change.

That being said, when differences between teachers and students are not psychologically destructive, they can provide an opportunity to learn. People do think and process information in different ways. To get along, we have to tolerate those differences and learn about those differences. Throughout the education processes, children will encounter a variety of teaching styles. This may be a time to work with an educational specialist who can teach your child methods for adapting.

The student with learning differences tends to have an uneven school career. Parents often tell us their child's first grade was wonderful and second grade was a disaster. As they get older, they hopefully will learn the strategies to compensate for their strong differences. Many of these children do better in junior high and high school than they ever did in elementary school due to the variety of teaching styles they are exposed to in these upper grades.

Evaluation

An in depth evaluation can determine a child's strengths and weaknesses, identify and explain different learning styles, provide an effective academic plan and later, may raise self esteem.

When to Refer a Child for Help

Consider getting help when there is a significant discrepancy in your child's learning ability and his achievement. If your child is known to be bright, yet not reading or not choosing to read, or is underachieving in math, get help. As much as people are reluctant to compare children to their peers, because there are so many differences in learning rate and learning styles, comparison can sometimes be a gauge of a learning problem.

When a child regularly grasps concepts a bit behind her peers, one of the things to examine is the parents' learning history. Perhaps this is a developmental style of a family who blossoms as students at later ages. Perhaps the parents first learned to read in the third grade.

Consider the seven-year-old boy with no interest in reading, but who was flourishing in science and math. Should there be an intervention or should the parents wait and see what happens? With a seven-year-old, the delay may indicate a lack of interest in reading. On the other hand, by the time he turns eight and his peers are reading fluently, he may feel they he is not as smart because he cannot read.

Children tend to define themselves as students by their reading ability. By the end of first grade, evaluate at what level your child is reading. If it is far below grade level, this is the summer to make an intervention and encourage developmental reading skills. You will still have a highly motivated student, one who has yet to experience a major failure. Provide your child with learning strategies.

However, we caution you not to subject your child to endless testing. A specialist can provide an academic screening of baseline information about your child's level of reading, reading comprehension, spelling, math, word recognition, word analysis (phonic skills) and vocabulary. A specialist will meet with you and ask about your child's learning development and make a decision about what testing is needed. Be selective.

A screening early on in a child's academic career can identify strengths and problems. Early screenings can provide good information about when or if there should be an intervention with any remediation, enrichment or tutoring. Because there are differences in rates of learning, and because it is impossible for a teacher to teach a completely individualized program to every student, supplementing school with good tutors can be beneficial.

Home Schooling

In general, we are cautious about evaluating the circumstances around recommending home schooling. There may be special reasons to home school on a short-term basis. Some special-needs children present requirements that cannot be met by public or private school. In cases where home schooling is necessary, curriculum stores are excellent sources for materials, catalogues or activities, as is the Internet.

School Placement Specialists

School placement specialists try to match you and your child with a school. Most experts will ask for direct contact with you, although some will send you packets and forms to be completed in your home. These specialists are familiar with the schools. Their recommendations will depend on their knowledge both of the schools and of your child. Often you will be given forms to fill out about your child's developmental, family and school history. You may be asked to supply report cards (up to three years), work samples, test scores, teacher observations, and an essay or writing sample done by your child.

The writing sample is evaluated on several levels and reviewed for vocabulary, syntax (use of grammar), and themes. The child should write the essay. You want the personnel to see the child accurately so they can make an appropriate recommendation based on your child's actual ability. A camouflaged child may be placed incorrectly.

Parents wonder if they should correct the spelling errors. Sometimes the answer is yes, and sometimes no. If this is information only to be seen by the specialist and not passed on to schools, then it can be used in a diagnostic manner. If the sample will be passed on to a school, you may want to encourage your child to proofread and correct as many spelling and grammar errors as possible. Some parents are tempted to write the sample for their child. We urge you not to do so, as it will be immediately recognizable as an adult essay, and not student work.

One specialist requested the following information from parents and child:

- Child development history and behavior forms
- A survey of developmental learning ability
- Written essay
- Application packet
- Report cards for the last three years
- All available test scores
- Teacher recommendations

Additionally, a specialist might ask for a paragraph written by the child about herself or she might be shown a picture and asked to write a paragraph about it.

For detailed information about selecting and changing schools, please read our first book, *Choosing the Right School for Your Child.*

Other Approaches to Diagnoses and Treatment Plans:

Possible resources to consult when you are concerned about your child's learning are:

- Pediatrician or family doctor for a referral
- Psychologist – Neuropsychologist
- University Health Center
- Psychiatrist
- Educational Consultant

SPECIAL EDUCATION STUDENTS IN REGULAR CLASSROOMS

Assisting Children with Special Needs

It is beneficial for students with and without special needs to understand who will be in their classroom in the future. Special education services in the public schools are divided into two categories: inclusion and mainstreaming.

A shadow teacher may be assigned to assist and follow the child in this setting. A shadow teacher is trained to assist a student, socially and academically, throughout the school day.

Mainstreaming: A special-day-class-student who is mainstreamed, spends a portion of the school day in a regular general education class. These students are assigned to mainstream classes based on their current ability level. The mainstreamed student is expected to meet the same objectives and curriculum requirements of the other students in that class. A shadow teacher might be provided to assist and follow the child in this setting.

Inclusion: If a student has an inclusion service, the plan has been developed in an Individualized Education Program (IEP). That plan is made in combination with the general education and the special education units. There is a possibility that the inclusion student may not be expected to meet the same curriculum and behavioral objectives as the other students in the regular class. The regular classroom teacher supervises that child's curriculum and progress.

Some special day-class students are included into the general education program for at least a small portion of the school day. Flexibility and expectations are built into the curriculum for the student who may or may not be required to meet the same standards as other students in the class. Students are commonly included into art and music at the first level. Depending on the student's learning profile English or math classes may be added.

Special Purpose Schools

When the traditional school does not work, parents might consider Special Education at:

- ◆ Resource Centers
- ◆ Special day classes
- ◆ Special day schools
- ◆ Specialized boarding school

OTHER RESOURCES AVAILABLE FOR CONSULTATION

There may be a time to consider seeking evaluations outside the school setting. The following circumstances may indicate a need to consult other resources.

- When the teacher questions your child's achievements and cannot answer or explain a lack of progress.
- When the local school site resources have not increased achievement.
- When your child demonstrates frustration with his school achievement.

If you work with an educational therapist or tutor, it is important to have a complete assessment and set appropriate goals for intervention. It is also a good idea to schedule periodic evaluations to determine when to stop because the goals have been met or because the academic progress is sufficient.

Psychotherapy

Psychotherapy may be appropriate when a child is experiencing problems such as the following:

- Dealing with family life changes (divorce, remarriage or death)
- Difficulty meeting and maintaining friends
- Chronic unhappiness and/or worry
- School avoidance
- Antisocial behavior
- Bizarre thinking or actions

Speech and Language Therapy

The ability to communicate through speech and language is present in human beings from the moment of birth. As a child matures, each of the following four components needs to be integrated in order for language skills to develop fully:

- Phonology (speech sounds)
- Semantics (understanding of words)

129

- ◆ Syntax and morphology (the grammatical structures of language)
- ◆ Pragmatics (meaning of language)

Speech involves the production of sounds in words and sentences. Language is the use of words and sentences to convey ideas. Normal language development requires two components: receptive language and expressive language.

Receptive language refers to the words a child understands, while expressive language refers to the words a child uses to communicate. When a child is older, she may be asked to explain what a word means in a sentence. When a child has integrated speech and language she can adequately and clearly communicate her needs, thoughts and ideas.

Factors that can affect speech and language development include a child's attention span, activity level, behavior, and play skills. Each of these elements can enhance or interfere in the development and ability to acquire language. Physical factors can also contribute to delays in progress in language and speech skills. These include chronic ear infections, undetected hearing loss, genetic attributes, physical symptoms (such as cleft palate, neurological disorders) and constriction of the Eustachian tubes due to allergies.

If your child is not speaking properly, not reading or is having great difficulty with early math concepts by the end of first grade, a speech and language evaluation is needed. This is the time to ask the school to do a basic screening or to have a private evaluation.

By school age, a five-year-old should be able to communicate intelligibly, although some sounds may still be developing. For example, a five-year-old who cannot articulate the "r" phoneme (sound) may acquire the sound by age six. Other sounds that may develop later are "t", "s", "z", and "l".

By age five, a child is expected to carry on a conversation, initiate questions, answer questions and speak in full sentences. Conversation should be coherent and understandable. A speech and language evaluation would be warranted if any of these areas appear to be delayed.

Consultation with a licensed speech and language pathologist might include either a brief screening or an in-depth evaluation of receptive and expressive speech and language skills. Speech and language therapy assists the development of academic skills including:

- Categorization
- Language visualization
- Verbal memory
- Word retrieval

There is a high correlation between the development of these skills and reading comprehension, writing skills and understanding directions.

Preparing for Entrance Exams

The Independent School Entrance Examination (ISEE) is a standardized test for applicants to middle and upper school grades. The advantage to students applying to different schools is that they need to take only one test, which will be sent to all designated schools. The student does not have to travel from school to school, taking exams one at a time.

The ISEE test includes reading, comprehension, essay writing and mathematics. Each school may use this test in a different way. Some highly competitive schools will only consider candidates with high test-scores. Other schools will use these scores to identify problems or to initiate further inquiry.

Case Study: Allison was an ideal match for the school of her choice. When the admissions committee saw her extremely low math scores on the ISEE test, they asked her to come in and take a math test that they had designed themselves.

After evaluating Allison's scores on their customized test, the committee recognized that this student understood the math concepts. They also recognized that Allison organized her work improperly, and as a result, she was making errors.

The committee decided to accept her under the provision that she work with a math specialist the summer before her entrance. Happily, Allison had a successful seventh grade at her new school.

Some schools might have read this test information and decided that Allison could not successfully complete their curriculum. This committee, however, understood that the candidate was a good match for their school, saw the red flag and was willing to use the information for follow-up.

Alternative Therapies and Treatment Opportunities

When a child is struggling, parents often begin an "odyssey." They go from medical doctor to alternative doctor, to therapist, to advisor, bewildering themselves with so much information that either they do not choose any course or they choose a course that is not appropriate. Whatever course you follow, whether it is a mainstream course or an alternative course, be sure that it is working. Measurement along the way is essential to be sure that the treatment is effective.

There are a number of controversial therapies and treatments for learning and vision problems. Parents may be vulnerable to questionable therapies, which promise so much. It can be very appealing to parents when someone comes along with a program that says that five flash cards every night for the next three weeks will make your child a math whiz. To quote the old saying, "If it seems too good to be true, it probably is."

On the other hand, we would like to present a few alternative therapies with which some people have had success. We do not endorse them, and some seem to be more successful than others; the crucial thing is to evaluate the effectiveness of the program for your child—not your neighbor's and not your cousin's. Research all of these alternative programs thoroughly before you embark on any of them.

Biofeedback—Biofeedback (Neurofeedback) is currently offered as an alternative to medication for treating attention deficit disorder. If you pursue this approach, review the literature carefully and look for solid evidence of its validity. Make sure you are dealing with a licensed, certified practitioner. Ask to see the license and where they did their training. Ask what kind of results they have had with children like your child and ask for references.

Optometric Functional Vision Evaluation—Professionals who may be overlooked as a resource include developmental optometrists. These specialists are trained to evaluate more than simply eye health and clarity of sight. They evaluate how to use eyes for reading and for visual-perceptual processing of information. For instance, they can measure such visual skills as eye tracking and eye teaming (how the eyes work together). They can also determine the following:

- Whether a person uses their eyes in a binocular fashion. This is how both eyes are used together as a team when reading and writing. Difficulties with binocular vision can cause double vision, tracking problems and eye fatigue, which may affect reading.
- How well the eyes accommodate from far to near (for example, looking at the board at the front of a classroom and then back to a paper on a desk).
- How easily the eyes move from left to right (visual tracking).
- Visual memory and visual perception.

Common questions related to vision and learning are: Does your child get tired when performing reading and writing schoolwork? Is the child not performing up to his or her potential in school? Corrective reading lenses may be prematurely prescribed when undetected underlying language processing problems may be the true cause of a reading delay. The child may have delays in phonics skills (decoding words). Also many times vision therapy is prescribed or recommended even though it may be an accommodative problem or a binocular vision problem.

In addition to or instead of lenses, a series of visual training exercises may be warranted. Often these exercises are done with the help of a trained eye therapist in the optometrist's office. Sometimes parents are encouraged to do these exercises with their children at home.

Some students find enormous relief with corrective lenses and are helped by vision training, but results are mixed. Some students do not report any improvement. One student benefited by improving her tennis game but not her reading ability. Other students, from younger children to law school students, have reported benefit. Usually, visual correction and training have the best impact when combined with other services such as educational therapy.

Although helpful for some, in our experience vision therapy often has limited benefit in the classroom. In any case, we recommend getting a second opinion. For example, if your child has an initial evaluation done by a psychologist or neuro-psychologist, who pinpoints a problem, the therapist may recommend a course of vision therapy to increase visual tracking ability, reading fluency, reading speed, visual memory or visual perception. Following the intervention, it is important to conduct a retest to see whether improvement has occurred.

Appropriate visual screenings and thorough vision studies are important whether your child has a visual-perceptual or a visual-processing deficit. Your child needs regular vision checks, and the pediatric screening may not be adequate. A more in-depth look is crucial, especially in the beginning school years.

Tinted Lenses, Irlen Lenses—Helen Irlen has identified an area of visual difficulty called Scotopic Sensitivity Syndrome or Irlen Syndrome. Some of the characteristics of this syndrome may include:

- sensitivity to light
- drowsiness, irritability and/or the need to get up and walk around after reading for short amounts of time
- quickly losing focus on the page
- eye strain
- headaches
- complaints that eyes itch or feel tired

Helen Irlen has developed tinted lenses that help people with scotopic sensitivity become more effective and comfortable readers. It also improves handwriting in some cases. It is important to go to a certified Irlen Center, because proper testing, to make sure that the lens color is the color that provides the proper correction, is essential. Merely purchasing a tinted lens may make things worse.

Although Irlen lenses may be helpful for people who have Scotopic Sensitivity Syndrome, they do not teach anyone how to read. They may make the written page more readable. Once the scotopic sensitivity is corrected, a student can take greater advantage of reading instruction. This approach does not take a great amount of time or money and the initial screening is quick.

Computer-Based Auditory Training Programs—These programs are designed to boost sound-symbol association. They may help with auditory and reading comprehension.

Sensory Motor and/or Occupational Therapy—Sensory Motor Integration Therapy is useful for the child who is subtly awkward. Children with sensory problems suffer from sensory defensiveness to sounds, to touch, to light and or to motion. These are children who knock over bottles and bump into walls. Some children have a hard time holding the pencil and have an unusual grip when they try to write. Often their writing is difficult and labored. Some children are tactilely defensive.

Sensory integration is designed to help an individual become more aware of his body. Some of the clinics look like elaborate gyms, and many of the activities, particularly for the younger children, are perceived as fun and are not threatening. For some, sensory motor integration therapy has translated to classroom skills in terms of writing skills. Visual training and sensory integration training may overlap nicely with each other.

Medical

Medical and physical health conditions can affect emotional well-being and school progress. Medical needs may qualify a child for special services. They may also require in depth assessment by specialists such as medical doctors, psychologists or psychiatrists. A significant discrepancy between ability level and current achievement level usually must be demonstrated before the school will provide special services. Intervention may be warranted for medical treatment in a number of forms. Consider having both a school specialist and an outside specialist (second opinion) evaluate the impact of a medical condition on the child's ability to learn and to navigate school life. Medications may need to be administered at school with the assistance of a nurse. Accommodations at school may be required. Keep your child, your child's teacher and your child's caretakers informed of changes.

The following medical and psychological areas might affect educational progress:

- Allergies
- Poor diet and/or health plan
- Medication side effects

- Sleep issues (poor quality sleep, drowsiness, insomnia)
- Attendance (missing school, missing the flow of a school experience or even a whole unit of learning)
- Inattention
- Comprehension problems
- Behavior problems
- Physical disabilities
- Visual or hearing disabilities
- Speech and language communication disorders
- Attention deficit disorders
- Mental disabilities
- Developmental disorders or syndromes (Autism, Asperger's, Tourette's, etc.)

Mentors

Mentors are another resource to advise you and your child. Mentors can be tutors, coaches, counselors, spiritual guides or friends. Asking people for guidance is often received as a compliment. In times of need, many people are willing to offer advice and assistance. Mentors can be wonderful resources.

Caretakers

In this age of working parents and the complicated schedules of all family members, many families rely on grandparents, aunts, uncles, nannies and friends to help with driving, childcare and homework. These caretakers are essential to ensure that children who need special services are able to receive them. These caretakers are often the ones to share information from the specialist back to the family and from the family to the specialist. When caretakers are paid for their services, they may believe that their job is dependent on the child's good will. Some caretakers are afraid to discipline appropriately. They are afraid to set limits because they fear they will lose their popularity with the child. This can be very subversive. Stay aware of these situations. Respond as a team so that care-taking is consistent.

We are frequently asked when to hire, who to hire and when to fire a caretaker. When you hire household help, be sure the candidate is in step with your moral values. It is important to spell out your guidelines so that there is a consistent plan for caring for your child. The following kind of question should be asked during the interview: "What would you do if...". The caretaker must understand that the responsibility is to you. If your child complains or your child is unhappy, this does not necessarily mean that the caretaker is not doing her job correctly.

When you interview a prospective caretaker, ask for a complete history, including all prior employment and personal family situation (married, single, divorced, separated). Here are some additional questions to ask:

- Does his or her family or extended family live nearby?
- Does he or she have children?
- How old are they?
- Has he or she ever been arrested, received a driving ticket, lost a drivers license, or been in an accident?
- How long has he or she been driving?
- Request a copy of their social security card, drivers license, medical insurance papers, residency card or identification card.

Many parents drive with potential employees to see how they drive. Some parents provide driving instruction with a driver training school, including lessons about seat belts and car seats, etc. Until your new employee knows the route to the various destinations, draw simple maps. Explain the rule of never leaving the child alone in the car.

In general, you can observe care-taking and nurturing styles so you can advise, "when you seat Josh, would you make sure he is securely fastened, that his food is not too hot, etc." A home video camera can record the household in your absence, but this is controversial, and in some states, it is illegal. Hopefully, no abuse will occur. Make unexpected home visits. Enter quietly, and just observe how your home looks and what is happening.

If you notice changes in your child's behavior, pay close attention. Investigate if your child suddenly clings to you more, or if your child suddenly complains about the housekeeper. If your child exhibits increased aggression at school, this could be related to a home problem.

The person who is helping you with caretaking needs to understand that being on time for school, for pick-up after school and for appointments is crucial to your child's well-being. Your child must also take responsibility for being on time.

Teach your child respect and courtesy toward household help. The same manners are expected to be used with parents, teachers and at other homes with household help.

Other Resources

A large amount of information and material is available to assist parents. There are professionals in every corner, along with classes, psychology books, mentors, guides and religious support services, all of which can help parents to have a greater understanding of how to enjoy their children and provide for them emotionally and academically.

CHAPTER 8

PARENT POWER

Chapter Highlights

PARENT-TEACHER CONFERENCES
> How to Prepare for a Conference
> Academic Progress for an Early Elementary-Level Child
> What if the Parent Conference is an "Ambush"?
> Academic Progress for an Upper Elementary-Level Child
> Areas to Review at the Parent Conference
> What If the Teacher and I have Different Views of My Child?
> How To Ask for What You Want at Your Child's School
> How NOT to Get What You Want
> Positive Confrontation
> Questions Commonly Asked During Parent-Teacher Conferences

PARENT POWER
> Requesting a Specific Teacher for the Upcoming Year
> How to cope with a Difficult Teacher
> Parent Traps
> What If You Find Out Something Negative About Your Child?
> Weekly Progress Report

Parent power allows you to voice your preferences in regard to your child's education. Knowing when to fight for your child's rights at school and when to keep the discussions at home is essential to her welfare. We will outline the etiquette of the parent-teacher conference and suggest when to initiate this all-important meeting. This chapter is designed to make parents aware of the importance of sharing their power with their children. When there is a problem involving the future of a child, the child must be involved in the solution.

PARENT-TEACHER CONFERENCES

Conferences can be initiated either by school personnel, by parents or by students. When you go to conferences as a parent, you enter that room as your child's advocate with all the collective beliefs of your own school experience. Be aware of how your biases and history influence your approach to problem solving for your child.

When the purpose of the meeting is to deal with a problem involving school-work, set up a plan beforehand to go through what has happened, what is wrong, and what is missing from homework or assignments. This plan should include suggestions for making up missing assignments so the student can go from feeling hopeless to feeling hopeful. The goal is for her to begin learning and to feel contented about school. You might provide a private bonus for completed work. In some cases all past work will need to be forgiven so the student can start fresh and go forward from the present day.

We believe it is imperative for children to attend at least a portion of any meetings that are about them. Conflict is a normal part of life, and experiencing conflict does not harm children. Feeling they have no voice in the process harms them. If it is not possible for your child to be present, bring a written statement from her. This empowers her and makes her feel she has a voice that matters. During telephone conferences put your child on an extension phone, if possible, and inform the teacher or administrator that you have done so.

How to Prepare for a Conference

The first step in preparing for the conference is to ask your child how she thinks things have been going at school. What does she think has been working particularly well? Are there any difficult areas? Your child's answers will give you your child's perception of the school day.

Questions to ask your child to help determine her progress at school:

♦   Which subject would you like to have all the time?

♦   Which subject would you choose to never have again?

♦   What are your two favorite words you like to hear at school?

♦   What are the two words you like to hear least at school?

♦   Is your last report card/progress report an accurate reflection of your work? If not, in your opinion, why not? What do you think you could do to change them? What would it take to get a "B" if you have a "C" or an "A" if you have a "B"?

♦   How do you feel about your progress?

♦   Have you made your best effort?

♦   What would you like to change about your approach to school?

♦   What would you like your teacher to consider adjusting about her approach to teaching?

Keep in mind that this is a self-report and may be inaccurate. However, you can use it as a gauge to measure where your child sees herself.

The second step is to schedule the conference. Make it at a time when you are unlikely to be rushed. If you see that the teacher has no time for you that day, it might be best to reschedule. You may view it as a "part one" conference. Make sure that you are given the proper amount of time.

While scheduling may be a hardship for you because of your workday, it may be a hardship for the teacher as well. In the past, teachers had to speak only with parents; now they may be required to consult with psychologists, medical doctors, nurses, social workers, advocates, education therapists, attorneys and may have to schedule separate conferences with divorced or never married parents. You may want to open the meeting by thanking the teacher for his or her time.

Allow the teacher to speak first and establish the tone of the meeting, since he or she probably has a set format. If the teacher does not offer much information, say: "Tell me a little bit about your impressions of Josh and how things are going." If it is difficult to get information from this teacher, start by asking questions such as, "What is the best part of Josh's school day? When do you see him at his best? When are the moments when you think he is at his weakest? Is there anything we can do as parents to support your goals for Josh in the classroom?"

For reading evaluation ask the teacher, "At what *level* is my child reading? What is my child's reading strength? Is my child decoding words without understanding what she reads? Does my child understand when she reads silently to herself but when she has to read aloud does she stumble over words?"

Try to get specific information about academic progress. If your child is getting poor math scores and you have not had an opportunity to see a test, ask to see sample tests, so that you can gain information. Notice what kinds of mistakes your child is making. Does your child understand the concept or does your child make mistakes in aligning math problems or making rows or columns?

Academic Progress for an Early Elementary-Level Child

If your child is in third grade and you get feedback that her reading level falls at the middle of second grade, this is the time to ask whether that is typical for this class. Find out what you can do to help your child elevate her reading to a third grade level. Ask if it is appropriate to get an evaluation to obtain more information about how your child learns and if it is time to get a tutor. Perhaps she needs individual instruction to learn how to read better.

Questions about math skills will vary. Taking grade placement into consideration, find out if your child knows how to add, subtract, borrow numbers, and regroup (carry). Ask if your child handles word problems and calculation problems equally well. Does your child use her fingers to solve problems and is that acceptable in class? Is your child afraid of math or does your child enjoy math class?

Additional questions could focus on your child's writing skills. Are her stories creative? Is her spelling wonderful but do the stories feel mechanical?

What If the Parent Conference Is an "Ambush?"

What if you arrive at a parent-teacher conference only to find other school personnel also present and an unexpectedly serious agenda? Open the meeting with a greeting. Ask how everyone is feeling and express surprise that the conference is populated with a large group of school personnel. Figure out what this is all about by determining what the issues are and where everyone stands on them. Find out what everyone would like to have happen at the meeting.

Take some control by taking notes. This demonstrates you are listening and also taking responsibility. Be willing to meet again if other issues surface. Agree to disagree, if necessary, and to postpone the resolution to a later discussion or to reach an agreement or compromise in the future.

This is a time for clarification. If you are confused express it by saying, "Help me understand this...I don't feel clear about..." Have a discussion to summarize:

- ◆ What was discussed?
- ◆ What was concluded?
- ◆ What action plan will be taken?
- ◆ What follow-up will occur?
- ◆ Who is responsible for each step?

Attempt to close the meeting with a positive statement such as, "Thank you for your concern about my child."

Academic Progress for an Upper Elementary-Level Child

There may be a shift in the upper elementary grades that is not publicized to students or parents. In the parent teacher conference, we encourage you to find out how assignments are given. Some teachers give them nightly, while others assign a packet of work on Monday that is due on Friday. It is thus left to the student to organize her week. Inquire about the procedure for turning in assignments. Suddenly, students may no longer be reminded to turn in papers the way they were in the lower elementary grades. It may be assumed that when an assignment is due, the student is expected to remember to turn it in.

Parents also need to determine how long-term projects are structured. Some teachers will provide structured guidelines for long-term projects, while others assume a child knows how to do a long-term project already. If this is your child's first long-term project, mention that to her teacher. More supervision may be needed, especially if your child is new to a school or has had a different kind of experience in writing reports.

If your child is overwhelmed by homework, it is important to discuss that issue at a conference. Determine how much time your child is spending on homework each night, then ask her teacher whether that is an appropriate amount of time or if it is more or less than expected.

In the upper elementary school years, students are losing their after-school time to hours of homework. If that is happening, consider presenting your concerns at a parent conference. Ask if eighteen problems of math are always necessary, or would nine serve the same purpose? Keep your tone to one of information gathering rather than accusatory, and remember that sarcasm can literally end communication.

Areas to Review at the Parent Conference:

- Does my child appear to try her best in all subject areas?
- How does my child do with long-term projects?
- Does my child need lots of reminders or is she working independently?
- Does my child comprehend what she reads? Can she now interpret what she reads and what she hears?
- Does she participate in classroom discussions?

- Can she respond appropriately on the short essay?
- Does she do well on sections that require straight memorization?
- Does her beginning essay work show organization of thought and logical deductive reasoning?
- Does she solve math problems?
- Does she get along with her classmates?
- What does the teacher consider to be her strengths and weaknesses?

One of the purposes of learning, and a sign of progress in learning, is developing the ability to study. Many children just do what is asked of them, but do not push beyond that point. Find out if there are areas that your child could be studying more and learning more about in addition to merely finishing and completing the assigned work. Helping your child learn how to study and review information consolidates learning into long-term memory.

Some teachers unwittingly slip into educational jargon. As parents, you may not be familiar with these terms. Before you go into a meeting, promise yourself that if there is anything said that you do not understand or are unsure of, you will ask about it. "Would you mind explaining to me what you mean by visual perceptual skills?" or "What does it mean when you say my daughter is an auditory learner?"

What If the Teacher and I have Different Views of My Child?

There may be a difference in your view and the teacher's view of how your child is progressing. If you think your child is not doing well and the teacher says everything is fine, do not get into a tug-of-war about who is right or wrong. Tactfully present your concerns, then listen to the teacher's view. Some teachers minimize problems because they want a child to appear in a good light.

When parents have a strong sense that their children have particular needs that may be unmet at school, it is important to pay attention to that instinct. First, gather more information. Then, if you think some sessions with an educational therapist or a tutor would be helpful, by all means follow through. It does not have to be a life-long commitment. If you do it merely for your own peace of mind, the effort has value on that level, because you will become a more relaxed parent.

That being said, parents can become overly concerned about their child's interim progress. A child may progress at an average pace or the right pace for her, but her parents may perceive it as too slow. This may lead parents to arrange unnecessary educational therapy or tutoring for their child. Enrichment and intervention can be beneficial or it can be excessive.

Be sure to discuss the situation with your child. If meetings occur with the teacher, have your child attend at least a portion of the meeting. This allows a child to express a viewpoint and to feel her input has value.

How to Ask for What You Want at Your Child's School

How do you keep your perspective if a teacher incorrectly assesses your child? How do you evaluate and deal with a "problematic" teacher, who has temporary control over your child's academic life? We recommend direct communication in the form of a parent-teacher conference, and we offer the following suggestions to help you get what you want without endangering your child's academic well being:

- <u>Be direct, clear and specific.</u> Offer solutions, more than one, if possible.

- <u>Follow protocol.</u> Talk with the teacher first. If appropriate, follow up with the principal, psychologist and/or district personnel.

- <u>Ask for a time-line indicating when services will be provided.</u> If appropriate actions have not been taken within that time-line or after a second request, go to the director and explain your previous actions.

- <u>Present the situation factually and objectively.</u> Avoid inflammatory statements such as, "She hates my child." "She has viewed my child as a troublemaker from the start." "I'm poor so I'm not getting the same attention as the rich." "We're different and we don't fit in." "You're only interested in the big contributors."

- <u>Make statements that begin with "I".</u> For example, start with "I'm hoping you can help. This situation is upsetting to me…" or "I've come up with some ideas…" or "When this happens, could you please notify me?"

- Express your feelings with non-accusatory statements. "I feel disappointed... or "I had hoped that..." are appropriate in this context.

- Avoid questions that evoke defensive answers. Avoid accusatory statements that begin with "You" or "You people."

- If you are not clear about an answer, ask for a restated explanation. Start your sentences with "I'm having trouble understanding this..." or, "Help me understand this, please... or, "This is a puzzle to me..."

- End the meeting by planning solutions. Make a plan, including implementation strategies. Agree to reconvene to discuss progress at a future date. Be sure to discuss the plan with your child.

How NOT to Get What You Want

- Complain—If you do not want to achieve your goals, complain and do it frequently. Make sure you never offer any solution. Make sure there is a whining tone in your voice. Complain to everyone but the person who could implement a solution. This technique might cause you to be a social outcast at your school.

- Bulldoze—Come on strong and unrelenting. Bulldozers know they are right and everybody else is wrong. They are pros at intimidation. They do their best not to listen to any other view.

- Tantrum—Throwing a tantrum also gets parents a "great" reputation. Tantrums may result in a mild respite, but they ensure that in the future, any request you make is unlikely to be honored.

Positive Confrontation

When you initiate a conference, you may want to use the technique of positive confrontation. Think of it in terms of making a sandwich using squishy white bread. The first layer consists of opening with a positive statement (Thank you for your time, thank you for your interest in my child, or make whatever quick positive true statement you can make.) Ideally, the child will be at this discussion.

Then you get to the meat of your statement sandwich. During this initial contact, try to bring in your observations. Use "I" messages by saying things such as, "I notice...", "That makes me wonder...", "I am concerned, I am wondering if you can help me..." This puts the teacher in a helping position. For example, say, "I notice that Jimmy has brought home two difficult math tests in the last two weeks, and the questions do not seem to match the homework that he has been given. That makes me wonder how we can help Jimmy in math." Next, wait for a response and hopefully, the teacher will give you some concrete information.

The third layer of the sandwich is to end with something soft by saying, "Again, thank you for your interest. "May we talk again?" Build in the accountability. Reiterate the plan you agreed to, saying, "This is the plan." "This is what I will be doing." "This is what my child will be doing." or "This is what you will be doing."

Then set up the next meeting, and ask the teacher to send progress notes, once a week at first but eventually diminishing to once a month. Keep the dialogue ongoing, whether by notes or by meetings. Formalize the resolution the best way that you can.

What if you follow this procedure using your best diplomatic skills, but the problem persists? Step two is to meet with a school administrator. When you contact the administrator, you might want to explain your concern. To present your case well, it helps to give the dates of contact with the teacher and to list what transpired.

We suggest you modulate your tone of voice. It is most effective to be informative not accusatory by using "I" messages that give information. For instance, you might say, "I have given the teacher such and such information." "I have attempted the following..." "I have had the following discussion..." "I am still concerned." "I now need your help." With this approach, you are giving someone an opportunity to solve a problem. You are neither whining nor complaining. You are asking for a resolution.

You may want to include the teacher in your meeting with the administrator and make it a round-table discussion. Sometimes, your child can stay for part of the meeting and then leave. When the child is not involved, it pits one person against the other or makes one the messenger of what happened. Communication may suffer.

Problems need to be approached cooperatively or they can become areas of triangulation. Triangulation means the parent and child are against the school or the school and the parent are against the child, or the school and the child are against the parent.

Case Study: Sara happily started sixth grade in September, or so her mother thought. The sixth grade teacher had a reputation for being tough, but Sara's mom thought her daughter was progressing well until she looked at the bottom of the backpack and found multiple homework assignments not turned in. She discussed the problem with Sara, who explained all her inadequacies of "I cannot write well, my work is not good enough."

Sara's mother immediately called the school and requested a conference. They went to school where the teacher, child and parent met together. Meeting as a threesome helped the teacher become aware of how she was being perceived and helped Sara feel less intimidated by the teacher's style. They concluded with an agreement of how Sara would be accountable for future assignments and not bury them.

Alternative Procedure: (Round Table). If you believe that you are not going to get a good response from the teacher, you can ask for a meeting with the teacher and the administrator. This needs to be done at the outset to prevent collusion. If you talk to the teacher alone, he might complain about you to the administrator, who might develop a mind-set about what you wish to discuss. The advantage to the round-table alternative procedure is that everyone hears what you have to say at the same time. Bring a pad and pen to every meeting and take notes about what each person says and what was agreed upon.

Second Alternative: If you have a good relationship with the administrator, you can go directly to him or her. Avoid using your meeting to criticize the teacher. Criticism forces the administrator to defend the teacher and takes the focus away from finding solutions and strategies to help your child.

Helpful Hints

Over the next few pages, we have outlined some questions to ask at parent-teacher conferences and included forms that many parents find helpful. Feel free to use these as guidelines to get the information you need and the responses that you want from your child's school.

<u>Questions Commonly Asked During Parent-Teacher Conferences</u>

<u>Academic Achievement</u>

Demonstrating competence in?_____

_____

Academics in need of improvement?_____

_____

<u>Social Development</u>

Lower Elementary School Students:

___Does my child appear to have friends?
___Is my child mostly working alone?
___Does my child work well in groups?
___Can my child work independently?
___Is my child highly sensitive?
___Is my child overly sensitive?
___Is my child well-mannered, following the rules of the classroom?
___Is there any way in which my child is disruptive?
___Is my child chosen by other children to be part of their work or play groups?
___Have you observed my child in the lunch area?
___Does my child eat and play alone or with other children?
___Does my child seek other friends?
___Does my child tease other children or is he/she teased by others?
     If so how does my child handle this?

Upper Elementary School Students:

___Does my child work well with other children?

___Does my child follow teacher directions?

___Does my child move easily from one activity to the next?

___Is my child invited to have lunch with other children?
    Is it with the same group every day?

___Is my child kind to others?

___Does my child understand the assignments and follow through
    with them correctly?

___Does my child need reminding to complete work or to start work?

___Does my child need prodding?

___Does my child work independently?

___Is my child proud of what he does as a student?

Additional information:_____

_____

_____

Emotional Development

Lower Elementary School:

___What is going well in class and at school?

___Does my child show pride in what he or she does well?

___Is my child overly sensitive?

___Is my child easily discouraged?

___How do I distinguish if my child does not know something that is required
    versus acting silly?

___What needs to improve?

___What has the teacher tried that has worked?

___How can parents and teacher remain allies and consistent in communication?
    What is the follow through plan from the meeting?

___How does my child handle frustration in the classroom?

___How does my child handle the interruptions that are a normal
    part of the classroom?

___Can my child wait to be helped? Does she raise her hand?

___Is she able to delay getting feedback from the teacher?

___Do directions have to be repeated?

___Does she need constant reassurance?

___How independent is she in her work?

___How does she accept not (always) being at the top of her class?

___Does she cry easily?

___How well does she separate from parents in the morning?

___Does she turn her homework in on time or must she be reminded?

___Does she remember her lunch regularly?

___Does she leave her jacket at school?

___Can she handle changes and interruptions as they occur? Can she handle transitions? Is she flexible?

___Is special assistance from the teacher required to help my child move from one activity to the next (in and out of lunch or recess or one subject matter to the next)?

Upper elementary school:

___Is my child motivated?

___Is he tolerant of others?

___Does he demonstrate sensitivity or insensitivity?

___Is he accepting of others who are not part of his inner social group?

___Can he work with others who are not his closest friends?

___Will he share information with others on group projects?

___Does he demonstrate a caring attitude toward others?

Additional information:_____
_____
_____

Behavioral Development
(Both lower and upper elementary school)

___My child's behavior is responsible, self-disciplined and takes advantage of classroom opportunities

___If behavior at school needs improvement review the following chart.

Approaches which are effective, adverse or something to try with my child:

APPROACHES	EFFECTIVE	ADVERSE	SOMETHING TO TRY
Time out/Time in			
Additional work			
Study hall			
Detention after school			
Detention during school			
Suspension			
Expulsion			
Immediate parent contact			
Accountability plan			
Homework plan			
Behavior plan			
Points as incentives			
Incentive plan			
Consequence plan			
Breakfast study club			
After school study club			
Other			

Additional information:

_____

_____

_____

How can the teacher make a positive contribution to the child?_____

_____

_____

_____

_____

How can the student make a positive contribution?_____
_____
_____
_____

How can the parent make a positive contribution toward the child?_____
_____
_____
_____

Plan for communication between home and school:

_____ Weekly progress report
_____ Contact by note
_____ Immediate contact by telephone
_____ Other _____

Additional information:_____
_____
_____

Things The Teacher Should Know About My Child:

Our family setting:

___Both Parents
___Single Parent
___Divorce
___Health concerns
___Siblings
___Age (old or young for grade)
___Other

Extra curricular activities:_____
_____
_____

Interest/hobbies/talents:_____

_____

_____

Goals:_____

_____

_____

Additional information:_____

_____

_____

PARENT POWER

Requesting a Specific Teacher for the Upcoming Year

When you have strong feelings about which teacher would be an excellent match for your child for the next grade level, make the request. But make it delicately. Go to the administrator or the current teacher or both, and describe your child.

Susan, a parent we worked with, made the teacher selection process successful by expressing her request in the following way: "My child learns best with project learning. I have noticed that Mrs. Jones does extensive project learning. Would it be possible for my daughter to be considered for Mrs. Jones' class? I think their styles match incredibly well."

School principals are often reluctant to change a child's class placement. Try to implement a plan that is agreeable to all. However, if your child is truly in a situation that is not being resolved, persist by meeting with the principal, psychologist and the teacher to develop solutions.

Make it a point not to sound demanding; otherwise, you may find your child placed in another class. Avoid making inflammatory statements such as, "That mean Mrs. Smith. I can't possibly have Amy with her. She will destroy Amy." Instead make a logical fact-based case for why you think your child will do well with a particular teacher. Administrators would be inclined to take note of the following statement. "I have noticed Mrs. Jones' style and how supportive she is with shy children. Being as shy as she is, Amy will blossom in Mrs. Jones's class."

How to Cope with a Difficult Teacher

What if your child reports that they are unhappy with their teacher? What if the teacher incorrectly assesses or grades your child?

- Ask yourself, "How toxic is this teacher?" See if your child can resolve things on her own after discussing it with you.
- For example, Heather said, "I don't like this teacher. She's mean to me." Her mother tried to get her into another class before getting the whole story. In fact, Heather felt she was not getting enough ribbons (prizes), and the teacher was excellent.
- Have you gone to school with your concerns? Parents often start with the parent grapevine or the parent network, which can be a wonderful source of information. It can also be a source of misinformation. Parents talk among themselves, some times with partial or false information.
- What can you do as a parent? Form an action plan.

ACTION PLAN:

- Gather information. Get the most thorough, objective information you can from your child. Do not wait. Waiting too long is the biggest mistake that parents make.
- Conference with the teacher.
- If necessary, ask an administrator to be at the meeting.
- Be sure your child is with you at the meeting so no triangle occurs.
- Come prepared with a plan.
- Document everything that occurs. Take notes and keep track of dates!
- Make the communication plan specific:
- When you will next meet?
- What will the teacher do?
- What will the child do?
- What will the parent do?
- How will the problem-solving plan be implemented?

If you have questions, go directly to the source. Most often teachers and administrators are relieved when they have an opportunity to correct misinformation. It is okay for all parties to express anger and frustration, but those feelings must be the springboard for action to resolve the hurt or misunderstanding. A good administrator

156

will make it acceptable for the teacher to express anger or frustration and will use that feeling to generate a solution.

Parent Traps

Case Study: Each time Avi complained about a problem, his parents quickly moved him from school to school. Wanting their son to be happy, they responded immediately, instead of evaluating the situations that made him unhappy and rectifying those.

Disappointments occur in every child's life. The minute a child seems unhappy, many parents rush to school to fix it. Though we feel for our children, often it is best not to interfere but to let a child take risks, face fear, fail sometimes and succeed sometimes. A child's pain of having to explain, "No I did not get on the tennis team" is an important life lesson.

Some parents "hop to" for their children. By immediately jumping to the needs of her child, Mom denies her daughter opportunities for learning how to cope with frustration or a new situation. These children see adults as servers and come to expect immediate gratification; eventually, they cannot delay gratification at all.

Here are some reactions parents need to avoid. We have included suggestions for more successful approaches.

♦ Immediate search and rescue—Every complaint is seen as an emergency. Instead, you could tell your child "That is a dilemma and we can discuss a plan."

♦ Fanning the flames—When a child says, "I raised my hand and Ms. Jones did not call on me," the following type of response from a parent would be unhelpful: "That's terrible! She must not like you. I bet she's playing favorites!" Instead, you could ask your child, "Can you discuss your feelings with Mrs. Jones? What would you like her to do instead?"

♦ Fear of taking on the parent role—Some parents become intimidated by the school process and/or personnel and also by their children. As the child begins the school experience, interactions with school may trigger a parent's memories of being sent to the principal or other negative associations.

- Parents may avoid confrontations out of embarrassment or feelings of inadequacy about their ability to handle a problem. A parent may not even be aware that this is where his discomfort comes from, and continues to avoid attending to situations until things become quite serious or until the school demands that they take action. Instead, you could say, "I had some difficult times at school. I would like to help you find some solutions to your concerns. Here are some ideas for us to discuss."

What If You Find Out Something Negative About Your Child?

If the teacher reveals something negative about your child or you receive a poor progress report in the mail, try not to become defensive. Sit down with your child and approach the issue calmly. It is helpful to use sentences that promote discussion, such as, "I received this progress report. Let's discuss it. I would like to hear your view. I would like to hear your plan for correcting the problem."

- Listen to your child's viewpoint.
- Do not get distracted by a thousand excuses.
- Write down the plan for going forward and how to remediate the problem.
- Become an informed parent.
- Follow the lines of communication at your school.
- Use some of the forms in this book as a reporting system between you and your child.

Weekly Progress Report

Your child and his teacher could agree on a form for a weekly progress report that is brought home daily or weekly to you for discussion with your child. It is generally your child's responsibility to circulate this report and gather the information. Below are samples of two effective weekly progress reports.

(Sample #1)
Weekly Progress Report

Student's Name:_____

Class:_____

Date:_____

Teacher's Name:_____

Demonstrating competence:_____

Assignments are current:_____

Assignments missing:_____
_____

Behavior progressing well:_____

Behavior changes needed:_____
_____

Test and quiz scores:_____

Homework current:_____

Homework missing:_____
_____

General Attitude:

Positive		Negative	
Attentive		Inattentive	

Teacher Signature_____

(Sample #2)
Weekly Progress Report

Student's Name:_____

Class:_____Teachers's Name:_____

Demonstrating competence?_____

Homework complete?_____

Homework due?_____
_____
_____

Quality of work is satisfactory?_____
_____
_____

Test scores satisfactory or above?_____

Missing tests or quizzes?_____
_____
_____

Positive attitude?_____
_____

Class contribution?_____
_____
_____

Behavioral improvement suggestions?_____
_____
_____

(Cont.)

Grade on test:_____

Grade on paper:_____

Grade on project:_____

Grade in class to date:_____

_____

Teacher's coments:_____

_____

_____

Parent response:_____

_____

_____

Student's response and commitment_____

_____

_____

_____

Teacher Signature_____Date_____

Parent Signature_____Date_____

Student Signature_____Date_____

Counselor Signature (Optional)_____Date_____

Director Signature (Optional)_____Date_____

NOTES:

CHAPTER 9

CONTRACTS
LEARNING - BEHAVIOR - DRIVING

Chapter Highlights

What Is the Best Way to Use a Contract?
What Makes a Contract Work Best?

LEARNING CONTRACTS

BEHAVIOR CONTRACTS
     Preventing Risky Behavior
     Mind and Body Contracts
     Responses to Mind and Body Contracts

SAMPLE CONTRACTS
     Mind and Body Contract
     Cooperation Contract
     Record of Daily Assignments or Projects
     Teacher Report
     Daily/Weekly Teacher Form for Report on Student
     Weekly Appraisal Sheet
     Home-To-School Report Form
     Student Information Form
     Cooperation Plan
     Television Contract

DRIVING CONTRACTS
     Sample Driving Log
     Learner's Permit
     Graduated Driver's License Rules
     Sample Driving Agreement (Long Form)
     Sample Driving Contract (Short Form)

Children want to feel they have some control over their own lives. A contract between parent and child can provide that sense of control as long as the child has a role in creating the terms of the agreement. All too often contracts address what the child is expected to do, with very little space devoted to what is expected of a parent. An effective contract has a balance of expectations.

Contracts with children work when they benefit both parties. Contracts do not work when the party in power (e.g. parents, teachers or therapists) creates the contract and every advantage goes to them. A contract that helps keep a balance of power has a greater chance for success.

What Is the Best Way to Use a Contract?

Contracts can be written for completing homework, watching television, getting ready for school on time, time management and many other areas. However, the child must clearly see the advantage to committing to this contract. For example, if the parent receives the advantage of having the teenager come home at curfew every week-night at 10:00 p.m., then the teenager receives a privilege, such as staying out Saturday night until midnight.

A behavior pledge could be written to obey traffic laws regardless of what other people do. This could apply to bike riding, walking, skateboarding, rollerblading and scooters.

A SUGGESTION: Have your child write a contract of safety rules as the bike rider, car rider, bus rider, etc.

Contracts that cover school success or a school plan may be between the following participants:

- Teacher and child
- Parent and child
- Teacher, parent and child
- Grandparent and child
- Babysitter and child

What Makes a Contract Work Best?

Contracts need a continuous process of review or renegotiation, usually every week or every 10 days. Post the contract on the refrigerator, in your child's room or anywhere that the contract will be highly <u>visible</u>. Otherwise, after an initial burst of energy, contracts fall by the wayside and then parents wonder why they do not work.

Contracts also need a time limit. Include a review date and a target date of closure or change of vision. Children become disenchanted if the contract is not reviewed or revised regularly.

Parents need to know when to stop a contract. When a contract has served its purpose, let it go. If necessary, you can reinstate it later.

Goals that are short, succinct, manageable and attainable are more effective for children than overwhelming and complex plans with a range of goals. In the case of a resistant contract signer, limit expectations to one goal per contract. For example, getting ready for school on time may be the subject of a single contract.

Here is an example of a learning contract. You might want to consider an additional incentive, a cash reward or a prize for accomplishing the agreement.

SAMPLE LEARNING CONTRACTS

Adam's Learning Contract:

* *I will follow all class and school rules and pay attention to my own work.*

* *The teacher will tap on my shoulder or wink at me to remind me to refocus.*

* *I will take time to do my most careful work.*

* *I will form letters and numbers carefully.*

* *I will finish my work on time.*

* *I will use my time well when working.*

- *I will try to notice and tell myself to focus.*

- *I will do my work by myself without bothering others.*

A good contract will address the following issues:
  - Accountability
  - Reciprocity (a mutual exchange of privileges)
  - An explicit plan
  - Clear goals
  - Continuous monitoring and reporting
  - Feedback and a reward (if that is necessary)
  - Closing date, review date, or time for renewal

A good contract will also outline how the parent will report to the child and how he will report to them. It will indicate whether there is feedback daily or every other day and who will administer the plan. All parties, not just the child, should sign the contract.

Contracts should be negotiated. For example, if your child asks for three dollars for every ten homework assignments completed, the parent might offer extra television time instead of money. Write the contract with your child instead of presenting a completed document. Letting him be part of the process gives your child the feeling he has the power to negotiate and is part of the decision. This approach prevents creating one more issue to rebel against.

For some children, contracts do not work. A child with a strong internal motivational system is usually not influenced by the offer of external reward. In fact, when a child is internally motivated, external motivations confuse her. You can tell if your child is of this type when she is working on a project such as building a castle. If you tell her what a beautiful castle it is, she may destroy the castle because you have interfered with her creative plan by giving your view of it.

The main goal of a learning contract is to help your child become a better student. Have her repeat the commitment and say back what she hears.

The following Learning Contract is more specific than the previous example and has some built in flexibility:

A meeting was held on Tuesday to discuss ways to increase study productivity and to improve the student's grade point average. Attendees were child (Darryl), parent, teacher and tutor. The following items were agreed upon:

1. Specific days of the week will be allotted for the review and study of the learning contract subjects.

Tuesday = Science
Thursday = English
Friday = Social Studies

a. These days may be changed if special circumstances arise; however, there shall be at least one day allocated for each of the above subjects.
b. Darryl will bring home the appropriate books and related study materials, even though he has no specific assigned homework.

2. Studying includes a review of the questions that are at the back of each textbook chapter. Darryl will demonstrate that he knows the answers.

3. Darryl will bring home all homework, and either teacher or tutor will check all math and English grammar assignments.

4. All graded and returned homework and tests shall be reviewed and analyzed so that Darryl can correct missed answers.

5. Darryl will keep a log of his assignments, the maximum score and his score, so that he is aware at all times of his current grade in each class. He will keep all returned assignments and tests in a notebook for ready reference.

6. *Darryl will review all math and English chapters that have been presented this semester in order to prepare for the standardized test.*

7. *Darryl will not answer the phone during the time that he is studying with his tutor. It is strongly suggested that he ask all of his friends not to call between 4:00 and 5:00 on all weekdays, so that he can devote his attention to his school work during these hours.*

8. *Darryl stated that his grade goals are as follows:*

> *Religion A*
> *English B+*
> *Social Studies A*
> *Pre Algebra A-*
> *Science B*
> *Art B-*
> *Physical Education B*
> *Computer A*

9. *Darryl will receive $10 for each grade that meets the goal. The total possible is $80.00.*

10. *Parent will double the monetary reward for good grades if Darryl succeeds in improving by at least one grade in each class.*

11. *Darryl, teacher, tutor and parent meet again in approximately one month to reassess the above and to review Darryl's progress.*

Please sign below if you agree.

_____
Student

_____
Parent

_____
Teacher

_____
Tutor

BEHAVIOR CONTRACTS

Preventing Risky Behavior

The United States Department of Health and Human Services studied the issue of risk-taking by teens. This survey identified ten risk behaviors and tracked the proportion of teenagers who engaged in behaviors including tobacco use, marijuana and cocaine use, suicide attempts and suicide thoughts, binge drinking and sexual intercourse.

Although the study indicated that numbers of teens were reducing their exposure to these violent and dangerous behaviors, a child who becomes involved with risky behavior may also associate with other teens that engage in these risky behaviors. Mentors, Big Brother/Big Sister organizations, individual and team sports, and family time present opportunities to encourage safe conduct.

Stay aware of the activities of your child and know your child's friends and their parents. Pay attention to any significant change in your child's behavior or activities.

As parents, you can reduce a child's risks from these behaviors by knowing about your child, caring about your child, talking together with your child, listening to your child, loving your child and staying involved in your child's life.

Mind and Body Contracts:

A Mind and Body Contract can offer a means for teenagers to avoid risks such as irresponsible sexual behavior, taking dangerous substances, fighting, or other inappropriate behavior. You may need to modify some of the conditions to suit your family's values.

Responses to Mind and Body Contracts:

Children who have made Mind and Body Contracts have written about their experiences, initial feelings and their successes:

"I have no intention of smoking, drinking or doing drugs at this age; however, if I were tempted by my friends I would be reminded of my 'Mind and Body

Contract' and it would help me stay true to my promise. I look forward to the day when I receive the money from the contract so I can spend it on other things and so that I can be proud of myself because I earned it. I would recommend this contract to other teenagers because I believe that it is a good motivation to do the right thing."
—Heather, Age 15.

"I am writing you to show my appreciation for establishing the Mind and Body Contract three years ago when I was 15. I can't even tell you how many times it has helped get me out of tight situations. Whenever I was pressured about trying drugs, tobacco or alcohol, all I had to do was say that when I turn 18, I will get over $2000 for not doing those things. All my friends I told this to said that if they had the same opportunity, they would also be drug, tobacco and alcohol free. I am very grateful you offered me this opportunity. You should really recommend this contract to other people that have teenagers. It really is an irresistible offer."
—Travis, Age 18, who earned over $2,000.

SAMPLE CONTRACTS

On the following pages, we have presented examples of various contracts that can work for your child.

SAMPLE
MIND AND BODY CONTRACT

I agree to keep my body whole, substance free and unmarred until I am at least eighteen years old. Substance free means avoiding all use of drugs (except for medically prescribed reasons), alcohol, tobacco or any substances of potential harm. I also agree not to pierce (except for earrings) or tattoo my body.

I agree that my parents have the prerogative to give me drug tests whenever they decide to.

If I decide to cancel this contract, I will first discuss this with all people involved in this contract. Otherwise, they can assume all is going well.

If I honor this contract, I will receive $_____ amount of money on my eighteenth birthday.

If I have broken the contract, my parents have the right to withhold the agreed upon reward, and it may be given to the charity of their choice.

I hereby agree to the terms of this contract and understand that you have my health, safety and best interests in mind.

AGREED:

_____   _____
Student/Child Signature   Parent/Relative Signature

SAMPLE
COOPERATION CONTRACT

Chris agrees to the following:
1. Care of the dog:
   - I will walk the dog at certain times.
   - I will feed the dog at certain times.
   - I will clean up after the dog.
2. If someone makes a reasonable request, I will follow it politely.
3. I will show respect to other people.
   - I will stop making up stories.
   - I will stop cursing.
   - I will stop singing in bed, if it disturbs others.
   - I will not disturb others.
4. If my friends come up with a foolish idea, I will not follow it.
5. I will have a nice attitude toward family members.
6. Regarding my room:
   - I will put dirty clothes in the hamper.
   - I will keep my room picked up.

INCENTIVES: My fish have been taken away because of things I have done in the past that were wrong. It is possible to earn back one fish per day by following all of the above. (If the fish needs a companion then two fish will be returned after two days in a row of keeping my agreement.)

CONSEQUENCES OF NOT DOING THE ABOVE MAY BE SOME OR ALL OF THE FOLLOWING:
  Loss of Privileges
  Loss of Stereo (Music)
  Loss of Television time
  Loss of Special Games

ACCOUNTABILITY: I AGREE TO TAKE RESPONSIBILITY FOR MY ACTIONS. I AGREE TO DISCUSS HOW I WILL MAKE CHANGES IN MY BEHAVIOR.

_____   _____   _____

CHILD'S SIGNATURE   PARENT'S SIGNATURE   DATE

SAMPLE
RECORD OF DAILY
ASSIGNMENTS OR PROJECTS

This is Sam's example of a way to have a daily assignment sheet of projects. Long-term notes are rewritten the next day or week if incomplete.

DATE:_____

CLASS	BOOKS NEEDED	ASSIGNMENT	LONG TERM TASKS
HISTORY			
SPANISH			
ENGLISH			
MATH			
BIOLOGY			

SAMPLE
TEACHER REPORT

_____ Working at grade level
_____ Assignments are all up to date
_____ Positive attitude
_____ Showing improvement/efforts in the following ways

_____

_____

_____ Socializing to excess
_____ Inattentive
_____ Assignments missing:

_____

_____

_____ Assignments not completed satisfactorily (state what is missing)

_____

_____

_____ Low test/quiz score
_____ Make-up work not completed
_____ Absences affecting grade
_____ Tardy to class
Teacher comments:

_____

_____

Parent response:

_____

_____

Student response and commitment:

_____

_____

Signatures:

Teacher:_____ Date:_____
Parent:_____ Date:_____
Student:_____ Date:_____

SAMPLE
DAILY/WEEKLY TEACHER FORM
FOR REPORTING ON STUDENT

Child's Name:_____

Daily Reminder
Date:_____

_____

_____AM   Great Morning

_____PM   Great Afternoon

_____Great Day!   Keep it up!

_____Morning needed to improve

_____Afternoon needed to improve

_____Whole day was difficult

_____Agrees to improve in:

_____
_____
_____
_____

Signatures:

Teacher:_____   Date:_____
Parent:_____   Date:_____
Student:_____   Date:_____

SAMPLE
WEEKLY APPRAISAL SHEET

NAME:_____DATE:_____

SUBJECT:_____
_____All assignments current
_____Missing assignments:_____
_____
Tests or quizzes on:_____
Project on:_____Due:_____

Teacher Signature:_____

SUBJECT:_____
_____All assignments current
_____Missing assignments:_____
_____
Tests or quizzes on:_____
Project on:_____Due:_____

Teacher Signature:_____

SUBJECT:_____
_____All assignments current
_____Missing assignments:_____
_____
Tests or quizzes on:_____
Project on:_____Due:_____

Teacher Signature:_____

SAMPLE
HOME-TO-SCHOOL REPORT FORM
WEEKLY EFFORT REPORT

Please rate this student's effort.

Name of Student:		Class Schedule				
EFFORTS	HM RM	MATH	HISTORY	LANG. ARTS	PE	SCIENCE
All Assign Current						
Missing Assignment						
Homework Turned in						
Homework missing						
Coop. in Class						
Class Behavior (Silly, Aggressive, Disruptive)						
Participates in class						
Non-participant						
Additional Comments						
Teacher's Signature						

SAMPLE
STUDENT INFORMATION FORM

NAME:

Changes in Medication:

_____

Needs:

_____

Medical Visits:

_____

Dental Visits:

_____

Injury:

_____

Good News: _____

_____

_____

Requests: _____

_____

_____

SAMPLE
COOPERATION PLAN

WEEK OF: _____

AGREEMENT   OBLIGATION MET

	M	T	W	Th	F	Sat	Sun
Up on time in morning, dressed and ready on time.							
Dressed properly							
Room organized and picked up							
At breakfast on time							
Backpack organized & ready							
Homework organized & ready							
Homework completed & done well							
No missing assignments							
Computer used responsibly							
In class on time							
Cooperative in class							
No dismissals from class							
Comply with rules & requests even if disagree							
Care of personal items (i.e. glasses, etc.)							
Opportunity to discuss feelings							
Organized							
Improvement Plan							

Student Signature: _____

Teacher's Signature: _____

SAMPLE
TELEVISION CONTRACT

Television Agreement Options

OPTION 1. Television viewing on weekends only or

OPTION 2. Limited hours of watching television during the week:

___ 1 hour daily

___ 1 1/2 hour daily

___ 2 hours daily

OPTION 3. Television viewing when homework is completed and done well.

When homework and responsibilities are completed how will free time be spent?

OPTION A.   Parents can decide.

OPTION B.   Parents and children can decide together.

OPTION C.   Free time can be decided by child.

What is the weekend agreement for watching television?

How much television do the parents watch? When do they watch television?

What is the policy of television during dinner?

DRIVING CONTRACTS

It is important that parents stay apprised of current and recent changes to teen driving laws. These laws vary from state to state. Different insurance companies also have various options and restrictions for teenagers.

More than anything else, teens need to log hundreds of hours of careful and supervised driving in the car. The new laws reflect this need, but parents are advised to take it a step further. Statistically, teenage drivers are far more likely than adults to be involved in car accidents. The arrogance of some teen drivers allows them to be oblivious to what adults have experienced in their years behind the wheel. Their lack of experience compounds the risk.

We recommend that you keep a log of hours on the road, such as the sample below:

SAMPLE DRIVING LOG

DATE	DROVE WHERE AND WITH:	NUMBER OF HOURS

Advance planning and driving agreements can save lives. The number of passengers a young driver can have in the car should be limited. It is also important for your child to read the car manual to help him understand car care and the workings of the car.

When your child reaches the age of fourteen or fifteen and begins to think about driving, it is time to talk about situations as you drive, handling dilemmas and safe driving techniques. Ask your child how he would handle these situations to heighten his awareness. One parent described her daughter's opinion of the rear view mirror. She considered it a cosmetic attachment to the car for putting on lipstick and combing her hair. Clearly, additional training and guidance were needed.

We have provided information and outlined some steps that may help your child safely navigate his early years on the road. Please consult the Department of Motor Vehicles Handbook for laws that apply in your state.

Learner's Permit

Most states require that an adult, aged twenty-five years of age or older, must always be in the car when the driver is driving with a learner's permit. In most states a student driver must have a learner's permit for a minimum of six months. Every opportunity to practice driving should be encouraged.

Graduated Driver's License Rules

Graduated driver's licenses slowly give teenagers more and more driving privileges as they increase their experience behind the wheel.

Step 1. Training that includes parent involvement and limits the number of hours a teenager can drive. Drivers education training either from the school or an outside institution is mandatory. Must drive with a licensed driver over twenty-five or a parent in the car. Drive under these conditions at least six months. Supervised driving hours (between fifty and one hundred hours, including ten hours of night driving) depending on the needs of your child. Drug and alcohol testing are at parent discretion.

Step 2. Pass drivers licensing test, age sixteen in most states. Drive alone during the day for several weeks to months until becoming a more proficient driver. Between midnight and five a.m. driving is restricted unless they are with a parent or an adult over twenty-five.

Step 3. At age seventeen, the young driver who has spent six months driving at the level of Step 2 and is free of accidents or traffic violations receives an unrestricted license.

As an initial plan for the beginning driver, or if your child has a driving infraction, limit driving time to days only for a month, then graduate to one month of driving days and nights. For any infraction the agreement should be twenty-four hours of additional supervised driving hours. If there is an accident, speeding or reckless driving, the privilege of driving for leisure should be reduced or eliminated, and only "necessity" driving should be allowed for an agreed length of time.

Driving privileges can be a condition on good grades. If your child is an A-B student, it is reasonable to expect A's and B's. If grades fall below C then car privileges can be suspended. *(Todd and his parents decided the passwords for his family about driving would be: No "B's", no keys.)* Some insurance companies offer lower rates for good grades.

Any high school student who takes on the responsibility of driving others must understand the need to maintain the car in good order. There must be seat belts for everyone in the car. They must understand punctuality and safety.

SAMPLE
DRIVING AGREEMENT
(LONG FORM)

I AGREE THAT DRIVING IS A PRIVILEGE AND NOT A RIGHT. I WILL DO EVERYTHING POSSIBLE TO PROTECT MY WELL BEING AND INSURE THE SAFETY OF PASSENGERS, PEDESTRIANS AND OTHER DRIVERS.

First Six Months of Driving with License:

___ Drive alone or with parent, no passengers.
___ No night driving.
___ No adjusting radio, CD or tape player while driving. Volume moderate
___ Driver's window slightly open at all times, in all weather.
___ No driving past midnight (If out past midnight, use a taxi, limousine, bus or call for a ride home.)
___ No driving on prom or graduation night.
___ No use of cell phone while driving.

We have the following agreement about the cost of car insurance: (Paid by parents? By student? Half & half? Other?)

_____

_____

___ I will renew the car registration promptly when due and get smog or any required certificates. Payment for registration will be made by:

_____

___ I will always have the required documents in the vehicle: current car insurance proof, current car registration, driver's license, and emergency phone numbers.

___ Car maintenance and repairs are the responsibility of:

_____

Repairs will be done as needed and following all warranty requirements.

___ Gas level in the car must not drop below:

_____

(It will be determined ahead of time who pays for gas.)

___ I will drive the speed limit posted and no more than that—or the speed that is safe, whichever is lower.

___ I will receive no tickets for moving violations or illegal parking.

___ I will get into no accidents. If I have the misfortune to be in an accident, I know that the following information is required:

A detailed written description of what happened as soon as possible after the accident (where, when, what, extent of damage, etc.) Get the name of witnesses. Always exchange information with the other party (names of the driver and passengers, drivers license, insurance, car registration, car license number also make, model and color of car.)

    Notify parents immediately
    Notify police as necessary
    Suggest keeping a disposable camera in car in case of damage.

___ I will pay for damages that are not covered by insurance.

___ I will pay for any tickets I incur and I will pay any increase in the insurance premium, which I cause, for as long as the premium is in effect.

___ If I am stopped by a police officer, I will handle the situation in the following ways:

_____

_____

_____

___ Carry emergency information in glove box, including names and numbers to call in an emergency. Carry a flashlight. An earthquake survival kit is highly recommended. This includes an extra pair of sneakers, flares, glow sticks, water, etc.

___ I can/cannot have passengers in the vehicle (first six months of driving after license issued). Passengers can be driven to social occasions, work or carpool transport only (or unrestricted.) The maximum number of passengers I can have in the car is _____.

___ I will always wear seat belts. It is a state law. There will never be more passengers than seat belts available in the car.

___ I will always lock the doors and keep valuables in the trunk of the vehicle or out of sight. I will keep windows and sunroof closed at night.

___ When in the slightest doubt, I will always give the right of way to the other driver or pedestrian.

___ The following is never allowed in the car under any circumstances:

    ___ Smoking
    ___ Alcohol
    ___ Drugs or illegal substances
    ___ Weapons

    ___ _____

    ___ _____

___ I agree to maintain the inside and outside of the car in a clean and neat manner.

___ I agree to the following behavior as a driver: I will be a courteous, well-behaved and well-mannered driver. I will drive responsibly. I will never race, show off, get angry on the road or be experimental, i.e. put body parts out the window or feet on the steering wheel). By driving in control I will be able to avoid an accident.

___ As a beginning driver (or if there are problems with the driving such as tickets or accidents) I agree that one of my parents may follow me in their car during the first month of my driving.

___ I will show my proficiency for driving on canyons, freeways, in the dark, with other companions, in heavy traffic, etc. by the following plan:

_____

_____

___ I will call my parents and notify them of my arrival at my destination at the following times (for example all evening driving.)

_____

_____

___ I will call before I leave to return home.

___ In exchange for the privilege of driving I agree to the following additional responsibilities: (For example, running family errands, care of a sibling, grade point average, trading for services, etc. Make sure the young driver knows that those responsibilities come <u>before</u> his/her social trips (e.g. going to the market or picking up siblings <u>before</u> going out with friends).

_____

_____

_____

Use of the car before and then after six months is restricted to the following times:

Before   After

_____   _____ Unrestricted use

_____   _____ Use on weekends only

_____   _____ Use for work or school only

_____   _____ Use of car varies with the following plan:

_____

_____

_____

___ The limit of the number of passengers in the car is determined by the seat belts or agreement with parents, whichever is less.

___ No loans of the car.

___ No other drivers may drive the car.

___ Under the dangerous circumstance that someone has been drinking, the rule about the car is: No designated drivers under any circumstance or only designated drivers approved by parents in advance. Safe transportation must be arranged.

___ Use of the radio is at medium to low volume at all times. The driver must be able to hear emergency vehicles and to concentrate. Headphones are never worn when driving. Never adjust the radio while driving. Stop to adjust station, cassette, CD, etc.

___ Car phones can be used only when car is pulled over to the side of the road. Car phone use is for emergency only. Never dial while driving. Car phone use is limited to:

_____

___ Remember that some schools offer carpool priority for parking spots.

___ I agree to plan ahead and never rush even if I am late.

___ I have reviewed all the driving laws and successfully passed all required driving tests and permits.

___ I agree to read the Motor Vehicle Department's handbook of driving laws *annually*.

___ Other considerations about driving and care of the vehicle are:

_____

_____

_____

_____   _____
Parent(s) signature   Date

_____   _____
Driver's signature   Date

SAMPLE
DRIVING CONTRACT
(SHORT FORM)

I hereby agree to the following rules and conditions in order to maintain my driver's license.

1. When operating a motor vehicle, I will never drink and then drive.

2. I will never use drugs and then drive.

3. No one will ever drink or use drugs in my automobile while I am driving.

4. If I am unable to drive for any reason, I will call home at any time, any place, for any reason. I will be picked up with no questions asked and no reprisals.

5. I will always use/wear my seatbelt. All passengers in my car will use/wear seatbelts.

6. I will make sure my car is always in good working condition. I will check gas, oil and tire pressure and wash the car.

7. I will always have my driver's license, car registration and proof of insurance in my possession when I drive.

8. I will drive safely and obey all driving laws.

9. If I do not comply with any one of the above items, I will lose the privilege of driving.

I agree that this will be a current valid contract between myself and my parents and I agree to abide by all the rules and conditions.

Driver_____

Parent_____

Parent_____

Dated: _____

NOTES:

CHAPTER 10

TRANSPORTATION

Chapter Highlights

CARPOOLING

Advantages, Disadvantages and Complications of Carpools
Etiquette
Rules in the Car During the Drive
"The Child's Okay, But I Hate the Mother"
Safety
Activities

GETTING TO SCHOOL INDEPENDENTLY

For many children their school day begins with the sound of a car horn honking outside their door. The tone for the rest of day is often set for them by that ride to school. As a parent, transporting a child to and from school can either be fun—or misery.

This chapter focuses on carpooling. Issues include the social advantages of carpooling, setting ground rules for the carpool, problems of punctuality, handling disputes, dealing with problem drivers and leaving a carpool gracefully. Faced with an older child who craves independence parents are advised at what age, chronologically and emotionally, the student should be allowed to walk, ride a bike or drive to school without an adult.

CARPOOLING

A unique mix of personalities and ages can make carpooling a challenge. Certainly, it is a cooperative adventure in tolerance. Some people have a tendency to be late, while others arrive early; some are highly organized and some disorganized. The ride home can bolster the good times of the day or dampen its successes or triumphs. For these reasons, we offer guidelines to help make your child's carpool life both positive and fun.

Before the school year starts, we recommend that you schedule a short meeting at one of the carpool family homes. A face-to-face meeting is usually better than a telephone conference. Prepare a list of things to be covered.

Many families develop a sense of group spirit by giving the carpool a name. Make it friendly, but stick to plans that are agreed upon in advance. It will make carpooling a much more comfortable experience.

Advantages, Disadvantages and Complications of Carpools

Carpooling offers many positive aspects besides easing schedules for parents. When a child has trouble with separation, being with other children in a carpool may help the transition from home to school. It is nice to have a mix of ages; older children can be supportive of the younger ones, while younger members offer the older ones a sense of responsibility.

Car pool members often have varying after-school schedules, which can create complications. Angie is on swim team. Aaron goes to soccer. Molly has to be home to practice piano. Before the actual carpooling begins, discuss after-school schedules. Some parents use different morning and afternoon carpools. For example, the morning carpool may consist of families who live near each other, while the afternoon carpool might be activity based, such as a soccer team carpool.

The highest priority is for each family to tell every other driver what to do if the family caretaker or parent is not at home. A list of pertinent numbers should be kept in each carpool car.

Case Study: One of the carpool fathers picked up a child from kindergarten and drove him home. Unexpectedly, no one was there and the father did not know what to do. He had to drive his own child to a baseball practice, so he took this five-year-old with him. He left a note at the house but the parents of the other child did not find the note when they arrived home. Panicking, they made calls all over. They were angry with the carpool parent for taking their child with him. However, his choices were limited; he could not stay at their house and wait, and he could not leave the child by himself.

Issues like these need to be discussed and resolved before carpooling ever begins. Be sure to clarify the arrangements and procedure in case you bring a child home and nobody is there, including:

- How a parent can be reached
- What is the telephone-tree progression? (Pager to mother, phone number at work, caretaker's number, etc.)
- What is the backup plan for telephoning and notifying a parent if no one is at home?

Make a contingency plan in case your child is sick or you have an emergency on your day to drive. Who can you call when you cannot drive? How much notice do you need to give them?

Address the issue of fairness: if you have more than one child in the carpool, does that mean you automatically drive two days instead of one? These questions need to be answered before the school year begins.

In case of an emergency at school (illness, injury or natural disaster,), make sure each carpool driver has permission to pick up the other children in the carpool families. Keep this information on file in each student's emergency records in the school office, along with a list of the carpool drivers. If there are any changes, update this file immediately.

Etiquette

Greetings and salutations can set the tone for reunions and departures. Children should be made aware of the courtesy of saying *thank you* to the driver each day. It is helpful to use this opportunity to teach appreciation.

What do you do when you are driving and suddenly you have one or two children arguing in the back seat? If at all possible, pull over to the side of the road and sit quietly. Hopefully your silence will gain the screamer's attention. You can say, "I would love to drive home. I am able to do that when there is some degree of calm in this car. I am not able to drive safely if there is this much noise."

If the same two children fight consistently, call a carpool meeting. There needs to be a way to separate two children who consistently do not get along. Setting up a system can reduce conflict and friction. For instance, you could set up a system where the child of the driver sits in the front seat, agree on a general rotation plan or create a seating rotation log.

Some carpools have different rules for each car. Children need to learn to respect you and your car. What is your policy for eating in the car and disposal of trash? Some drivers prefer not to have anyone eat in the car. Some drivers will take children for a snack on the way home. Some will provide snacks in the car. If you provide snacks in the car, make absolutely certain that each student is responsible for cleaning up his mess. Have a trash bag available. This is another topic that needs to be addressed at the first carpool meeting.

Is it okay to stop and do errands on the way home? This is usually a bad idea, since after-school activities and homework schedules may be tight, and variations can create additional problems. Be sure to make an agreement at the carpool meeting.

You may have set a rule that a carpool leaves a certain house at a certain time, but what do you do when you have a child who does not want to get in the car in the morning? Stay calm and explain to the child that you need to get to school. Encourage him into the car by saying you would love to have him with you. If you cannot prevail, then it becomes the home parent's responsibility to deal with it. You cannot make all the children late because of one child's difficulty. If you feel very kindly to the family, you might come back at another time so the child gets to know you. You may want to have him sit in your car while you are on the driveway so that he is familiar with you and your car.

If a child is not ready when you arrive for pick up, gently say, "Oh my goodness, it is 7:22, we have exactly three more minutes and I need to be gone." Pretend you are a train or a bus and you run on schedule. Of course, emergencies will arise to which you can be responsive, but very often there are families who tend to run late. The only way to cure them is to stick with your schedule.

Punctuality problems create challenges whether the driver is late or a child is late. If there are driver punctuality issues to resolve, an older student could attempt to talk to the driver and explain the dilemma in terms the driver can relate to. One case was resolved this way: "Could you pick me up a few minutes early? I was late to my adviser meeting every morning last week and my grade is going to go down one half point if I am late again. It counts as a tardy each time and will show up on my citizenship report."

If that approach is not effective and there is no immediate response, then the parent needs to call the driver. Again offer a solution or ask if there is anything you can do. One parent said, "My daughter is quite upset. She loves driving with you but she hates being late." If a driver is late too often, you may need to drop that person from the carpool.

What do you do if a child changes the plans but you have not heard anything about it from the parent? Since you are the responsible adult, use your list of phone numbers to track down someone who has responsibility and confirm the plans. If that is not possible, make your best judgment.

Watch for an unauthorized change in schedule. For example, one seventh-grade girl told the carpool driver to drop her off two streets from school for a dental appointment. Later, this parent discovered that she had inadvertently helped this child to ditch school. If a child wants to play or attend an after-school program or go home with another friend, the child must either produce a note or the parent must give approval in advance.

Rules in the Car During the Drive:

♦ Everyone agrees to cooperate. If there is a dispute, there is a prompt resolution, an agreement to disagree or a compromise.

♦ Students must check the car before getting out to make sure they do not leave any thing behind. If something of importance is left in your car, such as a backpack, and it is a one-time instance, do your best to return it to the child at the school.

♦ Celebrate occasions such as the first and last day of school, birthdays and holidays.

♦ Sing. This varies with families. Some parents are more tolerant than others of noise, singing and games. The children need to be respectful of the individual families and their rules. Books on tape that are age-appropriate might grab everyone's attention. For younger children, story and musical tapes are wonderful.

♦ Make it a policy for students not to compare grades and test scores in the car. If a student begins to do this, the driver can hold up his hand and say that the carpool agreement says no discussing grades in the car.

♦ Quizzing in the car can be educational or it can create problems. We know of one carpool parent who routinely tested the children on spelling different words. He thought this made the ride to school "educational." Instead, it increased feelings of tension and competition among his young passengers. However, some families have played question-and-answer games that focus on a variety of topics, such as vocabulary, history and geography. It works best if the level of questions ranges from easy to hard to encourage children of all ages to participate.

- Be respectful of the needs and uniqueness of each personality and temperament. Those who are not morning people are quiet in the morning and talkative in the afternoon.

"The Child's Okay, But I Hate the Mother."

If children or even families are not getting along well, one solution is to change carpools. Another approach is to consider this a lesson in tolerance; you can help your child to understand that carpool is a short part of the day and to make the best of it. The plan can be revised at the end of the school year. This experience can also be seen as an opportunity for a parent and child to bond as they survive the challenge together.

Sometimes the carpool does not work out and you need to make a change. This needs to be handled delicately. You may want to simply say that your family will need to leave the carpool. Do this only after you have made every effort to make it work.

Safety

A group of children were on the way to school in a bus. One father yelled out to the driver: "Be careful. You have $3,000 worth of braces on this bus."

Safety is no laughing matter. Even though you may be responsible about safety, other people may not. Check with each carpool member about his or her history as a driver, including the number of accidents and tickets on their record.

Substitute drivers may create anxiety for some children and their parents. Notify the carpool in advance of changes, particularly if it is a teenage driver. Do check with the other families before making a substitution.

We urge you to maximize carpool safety by:

- Making sure there is a seat with a seat belt for every child.
- Insisting that seat belts always be fastened.
- Avoid using a substitute driver, such as a Nanny, babysitter, teenager brother or sister, unless you have had a chance to gather information.

Activities

The policy regarding which activities are acceptable during carpool should be established at the initial meeting and written down. Of course, the driver always has veto power over choices of games and songs. In an effort to make the ride more pleasant, we offer up a sampler of games that can be played during the ride to and from school.

1.<u>Buzz</u>. You start counting and every time you reach a chosen number, (e.g. seven or a multiple of seven) everyone says "buzz." This game is for older children who know how to multiply.

2.<u>Herbie</u> is similar to Bingo. You can choose anything to be a Herbie. It can be a Volkswagen, a truck, a limousine or anything you are likely to pass on your way to or from school. The first person to spot five "Herbies" wins.

3.<u>Grandma's Trunk</u>. Start with "I went upstairs to the attic and there I found grandma's trunk. I opened it and found _____." Then the next person adds to that and says what the first item was too. The story goes from child to child, building the list.

4.<u>Related Words</u>. Pick a word such as horse. Then have each child say all the words that relate to that word or subject. Examples are equestrian, saddle, bridle, etc. Another example is house contents or a specific room in the house. Have the children name all the things usually found in that room or house. You could also use the vocabulary words they are studying in school.

5.<u>The Yes, No, or Maybe game</u>. The "questioner" tries to trick the "responder" into answering "yes," "no," or "maybe" to his or her questions. When they say it, they are out. So when you say, "Do you like ice cream?" and they say "yes" they are out. They could say: "I enjoy eating ice cream on a hot day." "What kind?" "It was chocolate" "Do you like chocolate?" If they answer "yes" they are out! This game also encourages language elaboration skills.

6.<u>Storytelling or singing</u>. Make up songs or stories about things that you see on the road, such as a horse, a taxi, a limousine, a person, a tree or a building. There are also sing-a-long tapes. Camp type songs are fun.

7.<u>Coffeepot</u> is a game where you chose a word that is a verb. Instead of saying the word you say "coffeepot" and you give clues about where you "coffeepot" and when you "coffeepot" so that the players eventually figure out what "coffeepot" refers to. It can get very silly, but it focuses attention on the structure of language. You could say, "I coffeepot every morning and every night." "My mother thinks I should probably coffeepot at school." Then, of course, they can ask questions. "Do you need anything else to coffeepot?" "Do you need equipment?" Hopefully someone figures out that you are talking about brushing your teeth.

8.<u>I Spy</u>. I spy with my little eye. The other carpool members have to ask you questions about what it is that you spy. It is a good exercise in deductive logic and questioning skills.

9.<u>Twenty Questions</u>. Establish an object by saying if it is animal, vegetable or mineral. Each person gets twenty questions in which to try to figure out your object. For a short trip, play ten questions.

GETTING TO SCHOOL INDEPENDENTLY

If your school is close by and your neighborhood is safe, an older child could be allowed to walk, ride a bike, or skateboard to school. It is a good idea to agree to a behavior pledge before school starts. This outlines the rules, traffic laws, helmet laws, etc., that the child must obey. Impress upon him or her that these rules apply regardless of what other children do.

Many states have laws that regulate the rights and responsibilities of beginning automobile drivers. Whether stated by law or not, beginners should not drive carpools for the first six months. There is a formula stating that it takes 100 hours of driving to become a competent driver. Even though a new driver can get a license before completing those 100 hours, some parents encourage their children not to drive independently, much less drive anybody else's car, until they have the recommended number of hours of driving under their belt.

Sometimes children want to drive before they are ready. There is often peer pressure to be a driver as soon as age permits. A parent's view and a child's view combined, of when they are ready to drive, is most important. How well trained they are as a driver is the most salient factor. Readiness to drive should be a series of conversations between parent and child. (Please read about Driving Contracts in the Contracts chapter.)

CHAPTER 11

ATHLETIC PROGRAMS AND EXTRACURRICULAR ACTIVITIES

Chapter Highlights

ATHLETIC PROGRAMS

Balancing Academics and Athletics
Evaluating Athletic Programs at Your Child's School
Sports Outside School, Club Sports and Organized Sports
From the Sidelines

ENRICHMENT PROGRAMS AND OTHER ACTIVITIES

Scheduling Extracurricular Activities
Enrichment Programs
Are You Living Through Your Child? The Over-Involved Parent
How Do You Decide When to Let Your Child Quit an Activity?
Field Trips/Outings/Overnight Excursions
After School Learning Programs
How Do You Evaluate Private Programs?
Television
Electronic Games and Devices

For many youngsters, athletics is a crucial part of their growth and development. Athletics may allow an exhilarating sense of mastery and achievement as young children learn new skills and improve others. Athletic programs may be especially helpful to students who have difficulty in the classroom but star on the playing field. A wonderful arena for practicing social skills, the well-run sports program allows a child to practice good sportsmanship and can give him a solid sense of belonging.

Extracurricular activities can provide excellent opportunities for your child to explore areas of interest not offered at school. These enrichment programs can also provide stress release as well as enjoyment. In this chapter, we will discuss when scheduling is appropriate and when it can become burdensome. We would like to remind parents that a little boredom can lead to creative play and imaginative thought. The key to successfully integrating these programs into your child's life is moderation.

ATHLETIC PROGRAMS

Balancing Academics and Athletics

Being part of a school athletic program is a good way to meet other children who may not be in the same classroom. It is a way of feeling connected to the school because school pride is associated with its teams.

Sports and athletics offer a welcome change from the classroom. This change of setting plus the physical activity are great tension releases.

A good sports program teaches self-discipline and the advantages of positive competition, while implanting the desire to strive for excellence. These skills apply to all areas of life.

That being said, we have strong feelings that children should be required to maintain a decent grade point average in order to participate in sports. This way, sports do not overtake academics, and students can keep their priorities in check.

Obvious differences in emphasis and responsibility exist between individual sports and team sports. Your child's age or personality may make him a better candidate for one kind or the other. *For example, as a young child, Heather hated Tee-ball but loved individual sports like ice-skating and gymnastics. Her personality was such that she was not inclined to be a team player until she grew older and learned how to be part of a cheerleading squad.*

Evaluating Athletic Programs at Your Child's School

Budget cuts have significantly reduced the physical education programs in many schools. Therefore it is even more important for parents to evaluate the staff, equipment and playing space at their children's schools.

What makes a good Physical Education (PE) teacher?

- Does the elementary school physical education teacher create a program that gets all the children interested and involved?
- Does the teacher give the students physical exercise that matches the child, being sensitive to the varying athletic abilities of the children?
- Does he or she keep a balanced program at all levels of capability?
- Is the teacher a participant, making it more fun for the children?
- Does she make sure that, in team sports, the two teams are balanced and that every one gets a chance to play?
- Does she make sure that no one is ridiculed for less ability?
- What sports are picked for the children to play? Are they fair for both boys and girls?

Encouragement is important at all levels! Have a balanced approach to encourage the children to understand how to improve and how to develop new skills. Positive, helpful words include "nice try," "good job," and "try again."

Sports Outside School, Club Sports and Organized Sports

Every year there are a few players who stand out, who have great athletic ability and who understand the concept of the game. These children are rare. While encouraging your child to participate in sports, do not MAKE him play, especially in a sport where he is weak.

Case Study: *Sarah was the younger of two sisters who played organized basketball. Sarah's Dad expected his younger daughter to play because her older sister had been a successful high school basketball player. Sarah played for one season amid tears and drama, and even though her team won the championship, Sarah hated it. The following year she switched to gymnastics, where she became a star. Now she feels happy and motivated.*

It is important to keep sight of the difference between school athletic programs and organized sports. Programs outside of school tend to become quite serious and competitive. Coaching at that level has a different focus, which is primarily to win. School sports are often more inclusive, depending on the school's orientation, and offer more opportunity for participation. This may change at the varsity and secondary level, but is typical at the elementary and middle school level. That is why middle school and particularly high schools set up junior varsity and varsity levels. The larger schools may have grade-level teams as well, which means there are three levels of performance at which a child may participate.

Parents should observe a sports program and see how it is run before enrolling their child. Remember that children do not possess the physical skills that adults and professionals have acquired. Do not expect more than the children are physically able to provide. Think of mistakes as opportunities for learning, not reasons for a child to be belittled or criticized.

In most cases volunteer coaches are as good as professional coaches, but it is a good idea to interview them. Do they make an effort to give everyone a chance to play? Are the rules rigid? If you show up, do you have to play? Are the teams balanced? Do the coaches encourage by making positive statements or do they belittle?

If your child has a bad coach or gym teacher, watch to see if the teacher lacks skills and avoids teaching. If you are qualified, volunteer to help one day a week to enhance the program. If the coach belittles children, talk to the coach first. Involve the child in problem solving. Gently suggest alternatives, e.g., "Could you tell Angie exactly how you want her to throw the ball rather than just tell her it was wrong?"

Little League Baseball: The programs can vary from team to team and from year to year, depending on the coaches. For the younger child, look for a Little League where everybody goes to bat and no inning is over until everyone has a hit or a turn. The leagues vary; some are more competitive and aggressive and some make sure everyone gets a chance at the bat. Some create all-star teams, while others try to establish a balance between stars and average players. Check the age and size of the other players to make sure your child is appropriately matched to the team.

Some parents become overly involved in these sports activities, and this can diminish the child's experience. Make sure your child is playing for his or her own satisfaction, not for yours.

Athletics can be rigorous and demanding and consume a huge amount of time, money and energy. This needs to be carefully monitored so that the athletic program is in balance with the rigors of school. If necessary, you can modify the sports program.

When helping your child choose a sport, the main criterion is that it should be fun. If your child is unhappy or uncomfortable, help her explore alternatives. She does not have to give up athletics and team sports; she needs to find one that matches her interests and abilities. Be sure that your child understands the rules to the game. She may need help from you to learn them. Some parents have been willing to draw a field and have play figures move around on the field. This gives children a game plan in their mind before they actually play and prevents them from having a horrible lost feeling when on the field. A good coach will often do this with young players.

From the Sidelines:

Parents play an active part in their child's sports. How they react from the sidelines impacts their child and the coach's view of that child.

If your child is upset after a game, here are some ways to respond:

Ask: "What could you have done differently?"
Say: "What will you do differently next time?"
Ask: "Did the children give 100% effort?"
Say: "You're the winner no matter what."
Say: "Do your best."
Say: "Be a good sport."
Say: "I had a good time watching your game today."

THINGS TO DO:

* Show your support and interest by smiling, nodding, and signaling a thumbs up when your child looks your way.
* Even when you are talking to other parents, keep your eyes on the field. Keeping your eyes on the game is a powerful way to show your support.
* Let the coaches and referees handle conflicts.
* Allow the coaches to control the game without comments or suggestions from the sidelines.
* After the game comment on specifics such as, "It looked as if you and Amanda were doing a great job passing the ball."

THINGS TO AVOID DOING:

* Screaming at your child.
* Getting yourself personally involved. It ruins the sport for the child.
* Telling your child what to do and how to do it during a game. Leave that up to the coach.
* Saying: "You're not trying out there."
* Saying: "How could you have missed that shot?"
* Telling the whole team they lost because they are not trying (In fact, some were trying and some were not. That's real life.)
* Throwing things (keys, clipboard, pencil, etc.)
* Wanting to win more than the children do.
* Saying: "Next time..." and telling them what to do. When you give directions to a child and tell him how to do it differently next time, the child may be left feeling demeaned. This does not empower the child. Let the child tell you what he or she will do next time and how they felt about it.

Encourage the other players to talk to each other and be supportive of each other. Encourage the children with constant support, whether they are winning or losing

ENRICHMENT PROGRAMS AND OTHER ACTIVITIES

Scheduling Extracurricular Activities:

While teenagers may be ready to handle, and indeed sometimes benefit from a full schedule, many younger children feel overwhelmed by an abundance of activities. Many theorists have suggested that the time children spend daydreaming and fantasizing leads to their ability to think at critical levels when they mature. In addition, children who have to make their own choices regarding activities become more independent.

Video games, soccer, ballet, gymnastics and music have an important place in children's lives, but the child who is programmed all day every day is expecting others to entertain him and does not develop his own resources. Motivation becomes external rather than internal. The child is at risk for a variety of disorders, such as stress, anxiety, apathy or burnout.

The signs of stress include:

- Resistance to the activity: "I do not want to go!"
- Stomach ache and headache
- Complaints about other children or the teacher in the program
- Acting out in the program
- Inattentive, distracting or inappropriate behavior

These are children who need unstructured, "down time," rather than one more scheduled activity. Even teachers who are subject specialists need to remember that their students have other obligations, which must take priority over an extra-curricular activity.

Case Study: Josh had three lines in a high school play. When Josh's mother learned he had a major test in biology looming, she decided to pull her son out of the rehearsal. Afterwards, she received a blistering phone call from the drama teacher, who complained that the whole cast was suffering because Josh had been picked up early.

Enrichment Programs

For the child who is not over-scheduled, enrichment programs can be wonderful and nourishing. In fact, for certain children, the activity may be the highlight of the week. For example, a child may be passionate about dance and live for that dance class every Wednesday afternoon, but he may attend a school that does not offer a dance program.

Enrichment also provides a wonderful forum for self-identity, particularly for the child who is struggling academically. It gives the child an arena in which to define himself, a place to shine and gain recognition.

Additionally, enrichment programs teach patience and delayed gratification. Participants learn that you do not become the world's greatest gymnast after two lessons or the best baseball player after one season.

Are You Living Through Your Child? The Over-Involved Parent

Is your child taking gymnastics five times a week because Mary Lou Retton was your idol? Are you dependent upon your child for your social activity? Do you look forward to gymnastics so you can visit with the other parents, or is this activity one that your child truly enjoys?

When a power struggle emerges over what a child wants and what a parent wants them to experience, that is a warning sign. Are the goals for your child to get some exercise or as part of a health plan; or are the goals to achieve what you or a coach desire? Children need to learn how to amuse themselves, how to engage in an activity that may not be part of the standard day, and how to put something special into their routines. It is crucial for healthy child development to know about activities in which he may not excel, but from which he gets great pleasure.

How Do You Decide When to Let Your Child Quit an Activity?

Many parents fall into the trap of viewing an enrichment activity as a future career activity. Children want to use enrichment for discovery and exploration. It is healthy for children to chose dance one time, piano the next and baseball the next. It does not mean they have not committed to anything. It means that they are doing exactly what they need to be doing in childhood. Exploring a sample of life teaches a child how to make decisions later on or to have the opportunity to say they tried many things. They will be able to laugh later about misadventures in tap dancing class.

A dilemma may arise concerning extracurricular activities. When the teacher says the student has promise but the child says, "It's boring, I do not like it any more," who makes the decision?

If your child wants to stop in the fifth week of a ten-week dance program, this may be an opportunity to teach commitment by insisting the child complete the course he has signed up for. Leaving the study of violin after the first or second year requires a discussion with your child.

Enrichment activities provide an opportunity to learn how to take risks. The adventurous child tends to become a more independent adult. Encouraging a sense of adventure makes enrichment activity a powerful tool. Some children are put into an activity and hate it throughout adulthood. The opposite can also be true, and some children develop a lifelong love or passion for that experience or retain a fond memory of it as an important part of their childhood. For some children, these activities become a source of esteem and friendships.

Field Trips/Outings/Overnight Excursions

The goal of overnight trips for children is to augment their experiences outside of the classroom. Some schools require participation in certain excursions to complete a grade. There needs to be an alternative for students who cannot participate in these excursions so they can satisfy the requirement. An alternative might be an athletic program or a research project. For example, if a class is going on a trip to Sequoia National Park and your child cannot go, he could research the history or geography or vegetation of this—or another—national park and write a report.

Many schools are forcing this issue. Some students may not be emotionally prepared for overnight trips. Others may not be physically prepared for the rigors of these trips.

If you do choose to have your child participate in these excursions, make sure you know <u>exactly</u> what type of equipment is necessary and whether your child is able to meet expectations. Investigate the contingency plans in case there is inclement weather. In one disastrous school outing no decision had been made in advance about what would happen if the weather turned bad. When a sudden storm struck, the children had to spend a night in the storm and then were brought home. A few of the parents were unprepared to receive their children who were expected to be gone a full week. In addition, many children returned home with severe colds and respiratory ailments.

Some schools believe that in adversity, a child will learn to bond with others. They may bond briefly in the difficult situation, but once home, things may return to status quo. However some children report that they enjoy the experience, even if there is some adversity. Twelve year old Simone expressed surprise that she could manage a hike that she thought would be too hard for her. She felt proud after she accomplished it.

New experiences allow children to explore different activities. While driving her children home from an overnight, one mother heard the children confess with embarrassment that they did not miss their moms and dads. They expressed surprise because they thought they would. Over-involved parents are often so fearful that they do not let their children go to camp. Children have their own fears and many miss the opportunity of going to camp because everyone involved is too fearful. By the end of the first day and night, most children settle in and enjoy the experience.

Of course, some children are too young for this experience. Our view is that fifth grade should be the first year of mandated overnight school outings; however, many schools start sooner. If a child is too immature or inexperienced at overnight trips, school trips can be unsuccessful.

Parents often ask us how they can be involved in the trips. Many schools do not allow parents to accompany the children. Some schools will allow a parent to accompany a child who has behavioral or learning delays. This is helpful to the child and does not limit the experience for the other children.

Advance planning for the trip is invaluable. Ask for a list of what to pack. Parents are tempted to embellish the list with lots of extra clothes and items, but it is best to stick to the list. Most children change their habits away from home. They may only shower when the counselor says they must. Forget extra pajamas; they will probably sleep in the same clothes they wore that day. Do pack extra socks, as they tend to get wet. Be sure the sleeping bag is the right weight for the climate. A Little Mermaid sleeping bag may be okay for an overnight in a home, but not warm enough for the great outdoors. If you cannot afford or do not have the things you need for your child's pack, let the teacher help find these items for you. Outdoor gear and sporting goods stores may rent sleeping bags and other equipment.

We suggest that you write letters to your child. Write at least two letters ahead of the trip so that your child will have a letter waiting on the first day. Send one letter each day from one member of the family, including the family pet. Make your letters short, and chat about what is going on around home. Do not say "I miss you." This implies that they should be longing for you. Instead write things like, "I'm thinking of you...", "I hope your day is filled with fun and adventures", "I will look forward to hearing all the stories of your experiences."

After School Learning Programs

After-school learning programs can compensate for subject matter that is lacking in the regular school program. When after-school learning programs take the place of the school, you may want to start looking at placing your child in another school. Some families are over-zealous in providing tutors and other supplemental programs for their children.

Carefully assess what you are using the program for and why. When after-school learning programs are used to give the child a competitive edge, this may be a symptom of a competitive mentality that centers around school or sports. Notice whether an extra-curricular activity is viewed as making the child competitive or better than the next person, rather than just making sure he has the basic educational skills before moving on to the next level.

How Do You Evaluate Private Programs

Businesses that offer tutoring services are proliferating, especially because of deficits in some school systems. The lack of confidence in our school system is startling: A news report published by Stanford University determined that only seventeen per cent of the population believes that our school system is effective.

A program that advertises extensively does not automatically qualify as a good program. If a program is expensive, it does not necessarily mean it is a good program for your child. Sometimes the wisest thing to do is to ask an educational therapist, psychologist, educational psychologist, or the school your child attends to do an academic screening of the subject area you are trying to improve. They should follow-up by writing a specific remediation plan of the educational goals.

When you sign on for a program, pick one that targets the needs of your child. For example, general math skills development may be mere memorization and not translate to learning that is applied later.

Before you commit to a program:

1. Ask to see the materials.
2. Ask if the same teacher will be working with your child each time. Some programs have rotating teachers and just as your child attaches to one person, there is a new person.
3. Ask to sit in on a sample session or have your child participate in a sample session before you commit to the program. Some of these programs try to make you commit in advance. Many responsible programs offer an assessment upon entry into the program and make a tailored education plan from that information.
4. Inquire about the credentials and licenses of the director of the program, the teachers and the tutors.
5. Ask how they train the people who are working there.
6. Is it a uniform approach that they are advocating? Some programs use a formula that is based on a theory. That theory may be sound but it may not be specific to all children. You know your child best. Does your child match this particular way of teaching?
7. Look at the facility. Is it clean, bright and cheerful? Or do you feel you are entering a dungeon? Have your child visit with you.

8. Find out if your child will be tutored individually or in a group. Some children can tolerate learning in a group and will progress in that setting. Other children need an individualized instruction program. Check on their flexibility. You may need someone to work one-on-one with your child. Some programs will accommodate this and others are so formalized they are not set up to do that.

Television

Television is both a plus and a minus. One way for students to relax is by watching one hour of television after completing their homework. The research is clear. Television can put you into an alpha brain-wave state, which is a relaxing state. The down side is that watching TV beyond ninety minutes often produces a stupor. Some people feel listless after watching TV and they do not always remember what they watched.

We think it is a good idea to schedule television viewing. Have TV days and TV free days. You might have a written schedule of who is going to tape which program and the time to watch those programs.

TV can be a wonderful source of information and entertainment. We recommend that you sit with your child and watch interactively. You can use commercial time to discuss what has happened. Do not be afraid to fast forward if watching videotape, or if you see something that you think may be controversial or inappropriate.

To teach your child how to evaluate a commercial, ask, "What are they trying to sell you and how do they think they are selling you?" "Are they using a pretty girl to sell a car?" "Why is everyone wearing white?" "Why do you think they use a certain song?"

Teach your child to critically evaluate what they watch on television. If you find yourself laughing at something, at a certain point after the show say, "What made that funny? I wonder why we all laughed at that?" Or, "What made that sad?" You can also teach problem solving to your child. For instance, if you feel that there was no moral lesson in the show, afterwards, ask your child what was another way to have solved this? What else could they have done?

Try to avoid becoming preachy when your child watches television. Rather than being judgmental about the shows she likes, find out what it is that she likes about the shows and why. This information can lead to insights about your child.

Electronic Games and Devices

Competition for status can motivate a child's request for the latest electronic devices, which have little inherent value. These are complex issues that create yet one more new arena for parents to learn about and to help their children distinguish between valuable and unnecessary luxury.

Parents are individual in their approaches to computer games. It is our viewpoint that the more violent computer games should be monitored closely and, in most cases, not be allowed. Most parents report these games increase agitation and aggression in their child.

If a negotiation is needed for study time versus playtime, however, the opportunity to play computer games, whether handheld or on the computer, can be leverage for parents.

When a young child is overly focused on wanting a new video game or device, consider postponement. Some parents have said the following to their children:
"We can discuss this at a set date." Example: Three months.
"We can discuss this on your birthday or on a holiday."
"There is plenty of opportunity to use that game at your friend's house." You can rest assured that a friend or classmate will be likely to have a popular game and be willing to share.

CHAPTER 12

FRIENDS AND CLASSMATES

Chapter Highlights

Helping Your Child Make Friends
Social Graces and Manners
Cliques and Popular Kids
Informal Clubs
Organized Clubs
Helping Your Child Face Adverse Situations
Bullies
Violence and Bullies
How Should Schools and Parents Handle Conflict
Strategies to Help a Child Cope with Peers Conflicts
Impulse Control

All of us have experienced the power of friendships, but the child without friends at school tends to see school as a sad and lonely place. The classroom is a laboratory in which to learn social skills and to practice how to get along with others. School becomes a wonderful place when it is filled with friends.

Helping Your Child Make Friends

When Maggie started her new school she cried everyday on the way home from school, lamenting her lack of friends. Her mother called the school and several administrators and teachers casually observed Maggie at lunch and recess. She appeared to be an enthusiastic member of a large group of girls. Maggie was looking for a "best friend" and had expected to have one very special friend from the first day of school. Maggie's story illustrates how each child (and adults too) define "having friends" differently. Maggie's mother had envisioned her at school, alone and isolated, without anyone with whom to talk or play. Eventually Maggie came to appreciate having a circle of friends and over time developed the closer relationships she so desired.

Conversely, there is Emily who talks about Morgan and Sam as if they are friends, when in fact she has no relationship with these classmates other than occasional hellos and good-byes. For both Maggie and Emily, the teacher's feedback about their friendships provides essential information that parents may use to help their children learn one of school life's most important lessons—how to make and keep friends.

If you are concerned about your child's friendships ask her teacher about how your child relates to other children at school. Does Emily eat lunch by herself? Is she a peripheral member of a large group? Does she sit with the same people every day?

Often it is helpful to ask the teacher to list three classmates that he or she thinks would be good candidates for a play date. Choose one person to invite, plan some activities and prepare to supervise. Some children benefit from a play-date rehearsal with you, their parent. Prepare your child for different possibilities, for example, ask Emily what she could do if Amy does not want to do an arts and crafts project. Are there any toys that Emily is not prepared to share with a playmate? If so, allow Emily to choose three things that she chooses not to share and put them away before the play date. As a parent, be sure that you have a series of "back up" activities that you can use at any time during the play date. Party books and game books are often wonderful sources of play date activities.

The following social skills are highly correlated with joyous friendships. If you notice that your child has difficulty with four or more of these skills you may want to investigate a social skills group for your child. A trained professional runs a social skills group. This professional models and encourages positive social interactions among the group members. Many schools are now offering these groups as part of their curriculum. Aspects of social skills that might be role played include:

- The ability to appreciate different viewpoints
- The ability to engage in conversation
- Recognizing body language
- Active listening skills
- The ability to accept compliments
- The ability to apologize
- Engage in cooperative play
- Asking for help
- Offering help
- Joining in
- Knowing how to greet and how to leave, "hellos and good-byes"
- The capacity to compete
- The capacity to lose with some degree of grace
- A sense of humor

Social Graces and Manners

Manners make a home and classroom civilized. Have your child write his manners plan. Here are some suggestions:

- Acknowledge people by saying "hello".
- Answer when spoken to.
- Be polite to everyone including family members, elders, and housekeepers.
- When visiting a friend's house, pick up toys/belongings before you leave.
- Use courtesy phrases such as "thank you," "please," "no thank you," "excuse me," and "may I."
- Put your hand over your mouth when coughing
- Use tissue, then put it in the trash.

- Always make eye contact. Focus on the speaker's nose if eye contact is difficult.

- When you call a friend's house say, "This is Jane Jones, may I please speak to Mandy?"

Cliques and Popular Kids

Cliques and groups of friends exist in most schools and anyone who has attended a class reunion sees groups and cliques reunite in an order similar to their school days. If your child is envious of the popular students, remind her that this may be the shining moment of that child's life. It also may mean that person is developing leadership qualities that will serve him well in socializing throughout his life.

There are a number of myths that children carry about the popular kids. One is: "Populars" are mean. Another is: I am not in the popular group and I think they are losers.

Some children are naturally charismatic. Some "populars" act elitist and alienate others who are not in the cliques. Many "populars" are generous, caring and warm individuals. Invite your child to individually evaluate qualities of each person in a group.

Help your child recognize that she can move to another group of friends. If she is one of the "populars" and feels too much peer pressure or is uncomfortable, suggest that she quietly befriend others and spend time with these new pals. If anyone asks why, she can say, "I am enlarging my circle of friends."

Case Study: Amy was not in the most popular group of students, but the middle group. Another girl, Mary, who had personality problems and difficulties, kept following Amy and interfering with her social development.

When Amy could not figure out what to say to her, I suggested saying something truthful, such as, "I know you would like to be my friend but that isn't possible right now. If I change my mind about it, I will let you know. But following me around makes me very uncomfortable. I know you have other friends. Could you please spend time with your other friends?"

It was an attempt to be kind to Mary and to minimize hurt feelings, but also to face the situation and not just continue to feel tortured by this child. Mary clearly was hurt, but she took it to heart, befriended other girls and has went her own way.

Amy not only learned how to take care of herself, but by being honest and true to herself, she also did a service for the other child as well. She modeled a positive and gentle solution to her dilemma.

Informal Clubs

Informal clubs are popular with some children. Heather tells about her club, which is called a Sanrio Club. Her friends have the same toys and they go together to share their toys and shop for new ones. It can also be made up of a group of friends with a common goal in mind, such as earning money for a trip to Disneyland or on behalf of a charity. In the process they could do good deeds in their neighborhood.

Organized Clubs

Organized clubs, such as school-sponsored clubs and church and temple youth groups are options for children to expand their social circle. These are different from self-defined clubs.

Questions about clubs arise if boys want to join a girl's club or vice versa. Girls are trying to gain acceptance to the boy's basketball teams and asking to join the Boy Scouts. Sometimes girls or boys feel left out of clubs because they often like to be included with their group of friends. Clubs should accept new members. This will avoid hurt feelings and expand their circle of friends.

Helping Your Child Face Adverse Situations

When teasing is done in a gentle, non-hostile way as a sign of affection, it can be gentle and loving. Teasing can also be cruel and have a powerful negative impact on someone's life.

Teasing often starts in the family. Some children misunderstand the subtleties of teasing and they get hurt. They do not really express the hurt because everyone has been laughing.

Particularly at risk for getting hurt, even by affectionate, gentle teasing, are those children who have language problems. These children are often extremely literal in their interpretation of language. They tend to miss cues from voice tone and body language. The comment, "Oh I was just teasing" or "I was just kidding" leaves a child with no defense. The object of the teasing has been wronged twice: once when they feel they have been put down and again when they are told "Oh she just doesn't get it. It was just a joke."

Teasing among children can manifest itself in many ways. Teasing can be used to get a person's attention. Children often want to be friends with the person they are teasing, but do not know how to be a friend or approach another child. In contrast, a verbally aggressive child uses teasing as a verbal attack cloaked in humor. Teasers like these often look around to see if anyone has been watching them.

Bullies

A bully is usually physically aggressive and/or uses the threat of physical aggression to intimidate his victims. Bullies often do their work on the playground out of the view of teachers. Both bullying and teasing are sniper attacks. These aggressors assume their victims will not report the attack. These attacks frequently come with threats not to "tell."

Bullies can vary in their approach to exerting their will. Some bullies merely want the attention of the person they are intimidating. They may be jealous or wish to be close to that person. A child who is smarter, better looking, more athletic, etc., may be teased out of jealousy or envy. Other children, who are smaller and/or socially or physically awkward, are easy targets for a bully.

Other bullies, who are more aggressive, consciously intend to exert control over the other child. They often have an ongoing personal problem with anger. They create their own reality and then exert their will to gain control. Because they are likely to be very determined, this type of bully is not someone that a child can confront.

A situation like this requires an adult, such as a parent, teacher or another authority figure, to intervene.

Ironically, bullies respect those who stand up to them. The minute you let a bully roll over you, he thinks he has your permission to continue on his course. The intention of a bully is to be malicious. This type of behavior may have its roots in jealousy or insecurity.

Some bullies do not have a conscience. They have a severe conduct disorder that will later develop into a serious adult personality disorder. When the victims of this aggresion are asked to draw pictures, they often depict people with lots of sharp teeth.

A child may not be able to distinguish between types of bullies. Having solid conversations with your child about their experiences with their classmates will usually let you know if problems are occurring. If a fight breaks out between your child and another child, investigate the incident thoroughly before you take action. It is appropriate to expect school personnel, i.e., teachers, aides and administrators, to be trained in approaches to resolving conflict with aggressive children.

Bullies may lie or tell stories to excuse or escape responsibility for their misbehavior. When adults believe them, this creates conflict for the child who has been victimized by the bully. It is important to find out if the victim of the bully was also contributing to the problem. Adults should spend extra time to reach the bottom line of the culpability, responsibility and solution. However, it is crucial to avoid blaming the victim for the bully's behavior.

Violence and Bullies

Everyone remembers an experience with a bully. It feels frightening and intimidating, and leaves the victim feeling mad or anxious. Confronting someone who is a bully is only advisable if you know they are not prone to respond with an even more violent reaction. In general, it is better to walk away.

Asking an adult for help may be the most appropriate action to take. Bullies often have serious problems that may not be evident to their own parents or to other children.

Regarding bullies, Bobbie told us:

"I can complete the case (meaning solve the problem), speak up and solve it most of the time, but sometimes the bullies are big and I can't solve the situation. I don't want to stress my mother, so I try to handle it myself."

Bobbie's mother appropriately explained that even if he was handling it himself, it would be helpful for her to understand his situation. She let him know she could act as his advocate if he wanted, or would be available to toss around ideas for solutions. In fact, Bobbie could not handle the situation by himself, and adult intervention was required.

Occasionally, a child can find the solution himself. Matthew told this story about a bully:

Case Study: "I was in Michael's class and I was writing something on the board for the teacher. Michael came over and pushed me out of the way. When he pushed me, my arm came down and the marker I was holding made a mark on his arm.

Michael yelled at me and said, 'Why did you write on my arm?' I told him I didn't mean it, but asked him why he pushed me out of the way. He didn't answer so I walked back over to where I was sitting before. He came over with a marker and he was going to write on me or push me or do whatever he was going to do. I had two other friends who came over and told him that he should leave me alone. They held him back. That was it for that day but he would keep bumping into me on purpose whenever he saw me.

A few days later, we were sitting in the back of the science room and he went up to the board and started drawing a picture of me, making checkers on my shorts because I was wearing plaid. Then he started making fun of my clothing. When he was drawing, I told him that maybe he should be the next Picasso. He didn't answer, but kept drawing. Then he walked away.

Since then, he really hasn't done much. He found out I really didn't care what he was doing. But he still annoys other kids.

The bully wanted a reaction and when he did not get the one he wanted he left Matthew alone.

How Should Schools and Parents Handle Conflict?

A number of schools do not address aggressive teasing directly and seriously, and the teasing is allowed to continue. In one school, a child had been allowed to bully and tease another boy for years by calling him "butterball." The result was lowered self-esteem in the boy who was teased, which had a negative impact on his self-image in later life. Teasers have an uncanny ability to zero in on someone who is sensitive, deep feeling, quiet and who will not make waves, "tattle" or seek help. The child who internalizes feelings is a perfect target for a teaser or bully.

We know of a school that instituted a program of conflict resolution as part of its curriculum. This program was set up by volunteers and run on a weekly basis. Conflict resolution, problem solving and self-esteem skills were taught at each grade level, starting in kindergarten. Within a short time, the school reported fewer instances of bullying.

Some parents of victims feel they should call the family of the bully directly. The risk is that the conflict might escalate into family warfare. Additionally, it leaves the two children involved out of the problem solving and deprives them of the opportunity for constructive conflict resolution. It is the children who should be confronting each other directly to do the problem solving.

Parents can do many things to support their children through the trauma of being teased or bullied. Immediate action is critical because when these situations continue unattended, it gives more power to the bully or the teaser and renders the victim more powerless, more introverted and more afraid.

Teach your child the body language that communicates "stop." Children can be taught to say "stop", "get away", or "leave me alone" in a very strong way. Often that is the only language the bully child understands. Body position and the power of the stance does matter. The shoulder should be balanced over the hips, both feet planted and leaning toward the aggressor, not away. Tell your child to position his hands close

SECRETS TO SCHOOL SUCCESS

to his body without clenching them, and to use a very strong tone of voice. Holding up his hand in stop-sign fashion and loudly saying "Stop!" also works well. However, if the problem persists, refer to the chapter on problem-solving.

If your child has to get help, he should seek the protection of an adult. Teach your child how to defend himself by being surrounded with other people and by playing where there is supervision nearby without appearing to do so. The minute a bully senses your child's fear, he is in more danger.

In serious situations, schools, principals and teachers should make a commitment to the child who is being teased. They must watch what is going on and intervene and help so that these children do not feel defenseless. When a child is bullied, his safety is threatened emotionally as well as physically. As parents, you want to take an active, vigilant role.

All too often, parents pull back thinking they do not want to be pests or considered over-protective. They tell themselves, "This is my child's problem, he needs to deal with it." In reality, this is a time when the entire family needs to come together. Let your child know this problem is real, it hurts, and help is available. Right away healing has begun. Discounting phrases like, "It will be okay", "Let it roll off your back", "Find other friends", leaves the child feeling very much alone.

Role play at home to learn ways of handling these situations and what to do when they occur. Teach your child how to evaluate the situation and not respond automatically. Discussion groups for older children can be helpful.

When a child creates a problem and the parent blames someone else instead, they can send the wrong message by leaping to the defense of their children too quickly. Parents who quietly help their children think through the situation, possibly even encouraging them to apologize and make amends for what they have done, give the right message.

Case Study: At sports camp, James bullied Matt over the course of several days until Matt finally fought back. At that point, the camp director became involved. He told James (the bully) and his parents that he would never be allowed to return to this sports camp.

At that point James's father began ranting and raving and berating the camp director. He then called Matt's mother with the same unrealistic views. The reaction by James's father charged the situation and changed the conflict from one that could be resolved in a meeting between Matt and James to one that left James with his father's confusing and unrealistic view.

Some schools have initiated "lunch-bunch" meetings, where a trained counselor comes in to meet with the classroom and then separates the students into smaller discussion groups. These meetings allow children to talk about strategies and ways to be with other people. It also gives them an opportunity to talk about what is happening to them in a supportive environment where they can get feedback about specific situations. In some cases, children may have an opportunity to confront their persecutor directly in front of a mediator who assists them and encourages them to speak the truth about their feelings. They can plan a solution or an action to make the bully accountable.

When there is no opportunity to confront the bully, there are other strategies. Write a letter to the bully using the problem-solving formula:

◆ Tell what happened (past).
◆ Tell how the child felt about it (present).
◆ Tell what they would like to happen next time or what they propose as a resolution (future).

There are two letters a child might write to the bully. One letter would be to ventilate the feelings; writing every venomous thought they had toward the person. This letter should <u>not</u> be sent. The second would be distilling that letter or narrowing it to effectively communicate his feelings. These letters cannot always be delivered to the bully. Sometimes there is an opportunity to face the person and talk about the situation.

Writing letters and, for very young children, drawing pictures, is a powerful and helpful action. They need to make one drawing of what happened showing the whole incident. Then they need to make a second drawing of a different outcome and a third drawing of themselves feeling safe afterwards.

When the letter or drawing cannot be delivered, one technique is to write the letter, and keep it some place where it is visible to your child. Every day for seven days, read that letter. After the seventh day, if your child feels better, you can have a little ceremony to rip the letter up and discard it. The idea is to finally let it go and release whatever feeling the bully created.

Another technique is to pile up pillows and pound that pile of pillows, since it would not be appropriate to pound the person. This provides an opportunity to aggressively ventilate the feelings and the anger.

Teasing can be so severe that it is contagious. The teaser looks powerful to other people, and weaker children may make themselves seem more powerful by aligning themselves with the bully or the teaser. There are some cases where you must take your child out of that particular setting and put him in another school. It is not always possible and not always recommended, but it is one strategy.

Strategies to Help a Child Cope with Peers Conflicts

Sometimes schoolmates fight, disagree or ignore each other. When this happens, have another friend try to help by talking to the two people in conflict. Get parents or teachers to help or stand by while each tells the other person her feelings.

When groups of children dislike each other and do not talk or play together, this presents a problem for a child who enjoys many different kinds of friends. In middle school she may get to see all groups of friends in her classes or walk to class with them. Some students when they see someone they dislike, they leave. A solution to the dilemma for the child who is friendly to both groups is to make a pact with herself not to take sides. It is best to avoid communicating viewpoints through verbal responses, facial expressions or gestures. It causes the person who dislikes them to put the child with many friends in the middle (a triangle) and ask her why they are disliked. It would be best to handle it by saying, "I'm not getting into the middle of this situation, you will need to speak directly to the other person involved."

Impulse Control

Children need to learn to inhibit behavior. To do this, they need parents who model how to be appropriate in containing thoughts that would be inappropriate if spoken. In describing impulse control, one child said, "It is about the thoughts I am thinking inside and then I don't say them to someone else outside."

Explain to your child that if we say everything we think, there will be considerable problems in the world. Thinking is different than acting. Acting on a thought can be useful and positive, but it can also be harmful and hurtful to someone else.

When teaching children about impulse control, show them what triggers escalation and how to de-escalate. Give them an example of something that might escalate an issue, such as saying that a person is an idiot. Then give them examples of statements that might de-escalate a situation such as, "We will talk about this later" or "That is an interesting idea, I will think it over."

There is also the option of ignoring a remark or action. Teach your child when to let an incident roll off his or her shoulders. This is not always easy. How we explain ourselves can be very important.

Here is a good example of how children can clear up their own misunderstandings:

Case Study: A boy named Chris stated that he was doing a really terrible job on a project. Intending to be supportive, another boy, named Rick, said, "I know what you mean."

Unfortunately, Chris misunderstood Rick's statement and assumed Rick agreed that Chris' project was terrible.

Chris got very upset, and Rick, who had tried to be supportive, felt very misunderstood. Rick decided to go home and write a note to Chris. The note said: "Dear Chris. I wanted to tell you that I knew how you felt about your project because I felt that way about other projects that I have done. You thought I was criticizing your project and I wasn't. I am sorry if I hurt your feelings. I hope you understand that it was just a misunderstanding."

NOTES:

CHAPTER 13

GUIDEBOOK TO YOUR CHILD'S SCHOOL

Chapter Highlights

STUDENT ORIENTATION—SERVICES—PROGRAMS
General School Rules
School Schedule
Events and Activities
Attendance Requirement
How to Handle Illness
Security System
Zero Tolerance
Backpacks and Lockers
Personal Belongings
School Pictures
Volunteering at School
Are There Fundraisers?
Students as Fundraisers
Alternatives to Fundraising
Library Services
Counseling Services
Student Records
Cafeteria
Physical Education Program
School Uniform Policy or Dress Code
Bus and Transportation Information
After-School Care and Sports Programs
Bicycles on Campus
Tuition Insurance for Private School
Student Charge Cards
Paperwork to be Filled Out by Parent
Newsletters
Electronic Communication—Use and Abuse

TESTING AND GRADING
Grading Standards, Honor Roll and Academic Probation
Exams
Standardized Test Results
Parent Teacher Conferences
How Teachers are Contacted
Homework Hotline

SUPPLIES AND MATERIALS
Restricted Items
Electronic Gadgets
Supplies to Keep at Home
Be Prepared with School Supplies

We encourage you to thoroughly review your school's Guidebook or Parent/Student Handbook, if they provide one. This is a checklist of important information to know about school policies. If your child's school does not publish one, we urge you to acquaint yourself with all school policies. To make you aware of the kinds of information that is helpful to know, we have listed sample policies, along with hints for adapting these policies and procedures to your own family's needs. A child is more likely to feel welcome to her new school if she knows the information described in this chapter.

STUDENT ORIENTATION—SERVICES—PROGRAMS

Orientation is designed to give students an overview of the school. If your school schedules an orientation day, family picnic or special kindergarten party, be sure to attend, as it will make your child feel comfortable at his new school and help reduce the "first day of school worries." Orientation will also familiarize parents with school procedures, such as where to pick up schedules or teacher assignments and how to locate classrooms, the lunch area, computer center, gym, etc.

On the first day of school, middle and upper school students will go to each class, meet their teachers, receive textbooks and begin their studies for the year. School orientation gives students a chance to get their bearings ahead of time and also find out the procedure for schedule and class changes.

For new middle school and high school students, topics often addressed are class schedules, available support services, required school supplies, availability of books, athletics programs, extra-curricular activities and school clubs. Orientation may also include an introduction to the administration, student council, faculty and staff, as well as a tour of classrooms, the gym, the cafeteria, and the library.

General School Rules

Is there a "Binder Reminder" or Student Handbook that lists the rules and procedures for your specific school? The following is an example of a set of school rules. A notice may be issued for breaking any of the rules.

- Be respectful at all times—no name calling, teasing or spitting.
- Show respect for authority.
- No cutting in line.

- No fighting, pushing or roughhousing.
- Eating is allowed only in specified areas.
- Gum is not permitted.
- Do not throw objects.
- Keep voices down in and near buildings and in the lunch areas.
- No toys or personal items on the playground.
- No obscene gestures.
- No vulgar language.
- No defacing school property.
- Walk in hallways and lunch areas. No running.
- Obey all playground rules.
- Obey all lunch area rules.

A handbook of schedules and assignment sheets should be available. If your school does not provide one, help your child make one. Include a cover page, identifying the student's name, class schedule, classroom locations, etc. Also include a multiplication chart, a ruler, personal directory of friends and study buddies, a planning schedule and calendar that covers September to June. Include blank assignment sheets for writing down assignments.

School Schedule

School hours vary for kindergarten, elementary, middle and high school students. Some elementary schools have one short day per week. "Back to School Night" usually means a shortened school day. Find out the procedure for schedule changes. For example, is there a set period of time after the semester starts when schedule changes are approved? Learn the hours of the administration office, the counseling office and the nurse.

Have a discussion with your child about the procedures if there is an emergency, either national, local or in your family. Have an understanding with your child about what to do, where to go, and back-up plans if the agreement goes awry. Sometimes schools have their own policies about emergency situations.

Events and Activities

Obtain a list of the dates and times of all school activities. Your school should maintain a calendar with school holidays, teacher in-service days, student free days,fund raisers, sports events, carnivals, parties, dances, school pictures, etc.

Keep a copy and incorporate this information into your personal calendar. Indicate whether the day is a student-only holiday or a family work holiday.

The following is a typical list of important days, excluding holidays that are religious or national:

- First day of school
- Back-to-School Night and Open House
- School holidays
- Winter Recess and Spring Vacation
- Progress reporting periods
- Report Cards sent home
- Last day to change schedule
- Carnivals or other festivities
- Teacher in-service days
- Picture day
- Parent conferencing periods
- Parent Teacher Association meetings
- Finals
- Last day of school
- Graduation Day

Attendance Requirement

Schools have a policy on absences and tardiness. Schools often lose funding if a child is absent. Students are expected to be at school unless they are ill or a family emergency arises. In its policy statement, one school incorporates the belief that when a child misses school, the child loses an important opportunity

Most schools expect children to arrive no sooner than ten minutes prior to their scheduled starting time and to return home promptly upon dismissal or the end of the school day. Check with your school to see whether adult supervision is offered beyond school hours.

Find out how absences are reported and recorded. Most schools request that parents call to report an absence, stating the child's name, the date and the reason for the absence. If your child will be out longer than three days, you may need to speak with her teacher. Attendance records should state whether an absence is excused or unexcused. Some schools scan the bar code from each student's notebook to determine who is actually present in school and who is not. If a student is not in attendance, an automatic telephone call is made to notify the family.

When a child has a communicable disease, a serious injury or needs to limit her activity, the school usually requires that she check with the nurse before returning to the classroom. If your child will miss school for reasons other than illness, for example, family travel or a family emergency, alert her teacher in advance so she can gather schoolwork for her to take along.

Other issues you need to ask about:

◆ How many absences are permitted before home schooling is required?
◆ How do children report back to school after an absence?
◆ How is tardiness handled?
◆ Are students allowed off campus at any time?
◆ Who is authorized to take your child off campus besides parents?
◆ How is a primary parent designated in cases of divorce?
◆ What are the emergency procedures for disasters such as fire, earthquake, flood or snow?

How to Handle Illness

Make a family plan in case your child becomes ill at school. When your child misses school due to illness, we encourage you to contact her teacher so your child can keep up with the work, if possible. Classmates might want to sign a get-well card for a child who has been sick for an extended time. Most teachers provide this kind of attention. If not, you could provide the materials and bring them to class so your child will feel connected and remembered by her classmates.

If another classmate is ill, encourage your child to call to say hello and ask how the child is doing. If the sick child is too ill to talk on the phone, have your child draw a happy face or another drawing and put it in his mailbox or tie a balloon on the door handle.

Hopefully, the worst illnesses your child will have are colds or flu with only a few days away from school. If your child has a chronic long-term illness, it is important that you immediately contact the school director and teachers. Let them know as much as you know and keep them frequently updated.

Learn the school's rules about illness. If the child is capable of doing schoolwork, what does the school expect? Some public schools provide home or hospital teaching for sick children. Public schools in Los Angeles City provide this service for a student who misses school for twenty-one consecutive days. Some private schools have limits as to how many days your child can miss before being required to repeat the grade. For example, some private upper schools allow a student to miss six days per semester. After that, they consider the student to have failed that semester. Some schools are using computer hook-up via E-mail to maintain contact with students who are chronically ill.

If your child is able to manage schoolwork, arrange to pick up assignments yourself or arrange to have them brought by a neighbor, friend or sibling. Many schools have the ability to fax or E-mail. If you do not have fax or E-mail capabilities at home, perhaps your employer will cooperate. Above all, make sure there is contact between you and the school.

Younger students who miss schoolwork usually can make it up easily. As your child gets older, missed days become a greater concern, both for the school and for your child. You may need a written report from your doctor to substantiate illness. Your child may worry about meeting a deadline for a project, being ready for finals, and completing long term assignments.

As soon as your child feels better, arrange a make-up schedule, if necessary, and identify due dates for work and exams. Be cautious not to overload a child who has been weakened by long-term illness, as a relapse may result.

Note the days when there is a nurse on campus, and learn what services are provided for accidents, injuries, or illness. It is imperative that you keep your child's emergency card current with information on how to reach you and/or alternate contacts.

Security System

What are the campus security measures? Who provides security? Will security personnel be on campus full time?

Parents might ask whether the security system checks all students or does a random check of a few students. There was an incident in a school where one child was caught with a dangerous weapon. The other parents were unaware that only a random security spot-check was made of students.

Zero Tolerance

Statistics on social trends show an increase in unacceptable behaviors in schools. Bullying, substances abuse, outrageous behavior, classroom disruption, physical and verbal abuse, and general disregard for the rights of others are all on the rise. Some schools have instituted a "Zero Tolerance" policy, which means a student does not get multiple opportunities to act out. After the first serious offense, the student is suspended or expelled.

Schools vary in their response to students who abuse drugs and/or alcohol. Many schools will automatically expel a student who brings drugs, alcohol or weapons to school. Other schools will suspend a student and demand that he or she attend counseling as well at a drug and alcohol rehabilitation program.

Find out what policy your child's school has instituted regarding substance abuse, safety, graffiti prevention, recess and lunch activities. Skateboards are not allowed on some campuses due to the risk of injury and helmet requirements. Certain administrators have banned some activities (current fads or collectibles) because these activities are viewed as inappropriate at school.

Children need to feel safe at school. They need to know that their classmates will be held accountable if they commit an injustice. Accountability is not a matter of punishment alone; rectifying a wrong, when possible, is part of accountability. Peer pressure is strong, but that does not justify misbehavior and damage. Schools that take action swiftly and firmly help children develop a sense of safety.

Backpacks and Lockers

A backpack is usually essential. Backpacks with wheels are appropriate if the backpack is too heavy for your child, especially if lockers are not provided. In some kindergarten and first grades, students are asked to bring certain supplies and then everything is pooled as a classroom resource. (See the end of this chapter for a list of basic supplies needed by grade.)

Have each child carry in their backpack or on their person a small laminated card that has the phone number where parents can be reached. Even though the school office has emergency numbers, it helps your child to know that she, too, can reach you at any time.

The card should state:

- Child's Name
- Parent's Name
- Parent's Telephone Number (Home & Work)
- Pager Number/Cell Phone Number
- Person to Notify in case of emergency if parent is unavailable

A backpack is an important tool for your child, but a private one. If you must look in your child's backpack, let her be present so it does not appear to be an invasion of territory or privacy.

By middle school, lockers may be assigned, and your child needs to be able to organize her things. Commercial shelving is available and can be added to a locker to increase organization. Adding a mirror (magnetic) and a grooming section may be important to your child. Emergency money for phone calls or lunch can be kept in your child's locker or backpack. Put the locker combination on laminated cards, which you and your child can carry, and also keep it in a special place so it can be easily retrieved in an emergency.

Personal Belongings

Students are encouraged to leave valuable belongings at home. Always put your child's name on the inside of backpacks, sweaters, jackets and electronic equipment, and on items for sharing. Label all student-owned materials in case of loss or theft. The "Lost and Found" is usually located in the main office. Save time by purchasing preprinted iron-on nametags, which can be sewn or ironed onto clothing.

Small children might want a secret bag with a change of underwear in case of accidents from nerves on the first day of school. Older girls may want to bring feminine hygiene products in a non see-through bag. They will know that it is there in case they need it, but no one else needs to know.

School Pictures

School picture day is usually scheduled at the beginning of the year. Make a note on your calendar so your child can choose an appropriate outfit. Tell her to smile naturally and practice, if necessary. If there is a yearbook, there may be a committee to work on it. Is it available to anyone? Be sure to purchase yearbooks early, as they are usually not available for purchase at the end of the year. Parents may be given an opportunity to volunteer as helper on school picture day.

Volunteering at School

If you can, join the Parent Teacher Association or Organization (PTA/PTO). Find out which parent organizations and school site councils are operative. Are there other links to the school and the community?

Working parents often have restrictions on their ability to participate. Schools are trying to respond by scheduling meetings very early in the morning or in the evening. If necessary, ask the school to make time accommodations.

Many schools encourage both parents to become involved, and several private schools have instituted a policy of insisting that both parents attend parent conferences. Fathers are increasingly seen as members of school committees and planners of school events. Some parents share a board position, either with another parent or as a husband and wife team. When divorced parents both wish to have a strong involvement, one parent can volunteer on the board one semester and the other parent the other semester.

Volunteer opportunities such as assisting in the library can be done occasionally or on a regular basis. At the teacher's request, bringing cookies to school can be turned into a major activity that is truly fun for your child.

You can sign up as the parent on a field trip, which is a service that is valued greatly by the teachers. If possible, attend at least one field trip a year. It is a golden opportunity to observe your child as he interacts with classmates and teachers and enables you to compliment your child on his behavior. Mention how considerate he was of another child, or how he helped to enhance the event for another child who was alone.

Are There Fundraisers?

What are the fundraising expectations? Is there a magazine sale, candy sale, wrapping paper sale, jog-a-thon or spell-a-thon? One school, for example, held only one fundraiser for the entire year. Because everybody knew they were not going to be asked to contribute to four or five fundraisers, such as having to buy gift-wrap, chocolates and laps around the track, people were much more generous. That school ended up earning twice what the other schools brought in.

Students as Fundraisers

Some schools encourage their students to actively participate in fundraising efforts that range from car washes to selling candy bars. For middle and upper school students, this kind of involvement encourages community and school spirit and gives a sense of personal autonomy and power. For others, most often elementary age children, the competition and pressure of fundraising may be discouraging as well as distracting. With young children, parents may want to help out by selling candy bars for them at their place of work.

Alternatives to Fundraising

Many parents do not feel comfortable asking others for financial contributions. Some parents are willing to contribute by sharing their talents. If you have a particular area of expertise but do not want to be involved in fundraising, offer your time to the school. For example, you can teach an art class or a computer class to other parents in exchange for their contribution to the school. Sharing your talent is a special opportunity to model true giving for your child.

If you are applying to a private school that is about to undergo expansion or building, the fundraising expectations may increase. During the application process, school administrators often look for people willing to become involved in fundraising. This means that you will be spending more of your child's academic and school life involved in finding ways to raise money.

Library Services

Learn the library hours of operation and when the librarian is available for research. If there is no library on campus, does the school schedule class visits to the public library? For secondary schools, does the school library offer computer access to other secondary schools, to university libraries and to the Internet?

Counseling Services

If your child chooses to use counseling services at school, are these services confidential? How are services obtained? Are parents informed? We suggest that you meet the school counselor first to determine if he or she is someone you would encourage your child to seek out for emotional guidance and support.

Student Records

The school district keeps records about your child. Psychological and/or special education case records normally are retained only until students reach their 24th birthday, but different districts have different policies. You have the right to inspect and review all records, files and data related to your child. If you have any concern regarding the accuracy or appropriateness of any information or records maintained by the school, you might discuss this with the school principal.

Accurate records can be important to securing proper services for your child. If you believe the district is not in compliance with federal regulations on this subject, you may file a complaint with the U.S. Office of Health, Education and Welfare. If necessary, a professional advocate can be hired to help you with bureaucratic problems. Whenever a student enrolls or seeks to enroll at another school, prior school records can be forwarded upon request.

Cafeteria

When is it open? What does it serve? Some school cafeterias are open before and after school to serve breakfast and after-school snacks. Do students purchase tickets or pay cash for lunch? What is the plan if a child forgets to bring a lunch? Are free or subsidized lunches available? If so, learn how to apply.

If the cafeteria is not utilized, pack a complete and nourishing lunch. Include a favorite food for the first day of school. Send along a card game like Snap, Go Fish or Old Maid or some other small toy which can be played with others at lunchtime; this is an easy way for your child to initiate relationships.

Physical Education (P.E.) Program

Physical education is usually required for all students. Determine whether physical education uniforms and/or special equipment is provided or if they must be purchased. Are students responsible for bringing towels for showering or does the school supply them?

One local elementary school has a P.E. rollerblading unit and arranges for students to purchase rollerblades from older students who have outgrown theirs.

Learn the procedure for excusing your child from P.E. participation.

School Uniform Policy or Dress Code

Are school uniforms required? If so, how can they be purchased? If uniforms are not required, is there a dress code? Must shirts be tucked in? Are specific professional logos forbidden because of gang affiliations? Are hats permitted? Some schools send home letters discouraging students from wearing certain combinations of colors because of gang associations.

Bus and Transportation Information

Does the school provide bus transportation? How is the bus schedule obtained? Where do you call to sign up? Remind students that bus riding is a privilege and certain standards must be maintained. Is there a late bus for students who participate in after-school programs, such as sports, debate team, yearbook committee, etc.?

After-School Care and Sports Programs

For young children, after-school care programs may be offered on campus or at another location. For older children, find out which sports are played at your school. Is special insurance required? Must you obtain a medical release from a doctor?

Bicycles on Campus

For some students, being able to ride a bicycle to school engenders a sense of independence and frees parents from carpools and bus fees. Find out how the bicycles at school are racked and locked. Remind children of the bicycle safety rules; bikes on sidewalks are always walked, never ridden. Protective helmets should be required. Follow and observe the right-of-way rules.

Tuition Insurance for Private School

Tuition insurance will cover unpaid tuition if students leave the school due to illness, or the school asks the student to leave. Tuition insurance usually is not available for lower grades, but frequently is available to middle school and above. Tuition may be refunded, if paid in advance. Some schools require you to purchase tuition insurance if your child is on academic probation, or if you pay on an installment basis.

Student Charge Cards

Student charge cards allow students to purchase lunch and school supplies without cash. Parent permission is usually required for their use.

Paperwork to be Filled Out by Parent

Keep up-to-date with forms which require parent signatures and information; these include student registration cards, emergency medical cards, and emergency release forms. It is critical that you completely fill out and return these documents. In a real emergency, you will want to be easily reached. One young student was not allowed to accompany his class on a field trip because his parents failed to turn in the permission form.

Newsletters

Many schools put out a newsletter to announce events. Will these newsletters be sent home and if so, how frequently will they arrive? One parent, unaware that a school newsletter was sent home every Monday, was shocked to learn she had missed several PTA meetings. After she and her son searched his backpack, she discovered seven weeks of undelivered newsletters.

Electronic Communication—Use and Abuse

Use of school telephones by students is reserved for emergencies or for school business only. Forgetting books, forgetting lunch, calling home to schedule going to a friend's house after school, are not considered emergencies.

Pagers are valuable tools for locating parents or children, if used responsibly. Knowing their parents can always be reached has a calming effect on certain children. To provide their children with a sense of security, some parents carry a pager.

TESTING AND GRADING

Grading Standards, Honor Roll and Academic Probation

What is the policy for passing a grade? If a child receives a "D" or "F" grade, can the grade be raised with make-up work? One of the things to check in the school handbook is grading standards, including what grade point average is necessary to make the honor roll. In addition to an honor roll, some schools have a separate category called a head master's list, which requires an even higher grade point average than the honor roll. Grades in certain courses, such as fine arts, may not be included in the averages. Your child may have A's in drawing and tennis but might not be considered for the honor roll, which is based typically on grades in core academic classes.

Determine the basis of academic probation and the procedure if your child is placed on it. Will your child be given a semester to be removed from academic probation, or will summer school or tutoring be necessary? If you have summer plans which conflict with summer school, offer to have your child meet with a tutor and then take an exam to demonstrate proficiency.

Finally, find out if there is a minimum grade point average required for participation in sports, clubs or student government. (Most schools require a "C" average or better.) This standard can act as a strong motivator.

Exams

Find out if there are policies regarding the number of exams given per week or month? Ask for an exam schedule, if one exists.

Standardized Test Results

Parents usually are apprised of standardized test scores, which measure their child's progress. Some schools have a policy of keeping these standardized test scores in the office and parents must request them. Some schools will not send them out and require a parent conference in order to get the scores. Other schools automatically send them to you.

The traditional and academically rigorous schools tend to place more emphasis on standardized test scores. Some progressive schools tend not to value these scores. Some schools send a cover letter to explain and interpret the test results, while some of the test companies provide an explanation.

Parent Teacher Conferences

Schools tend to schedule parent teacher conferences within the first few weeks of school. This is in addition to a back-to-school night, where teachers usually explain to parents what they hope to accomplish during the school year. This is a time for parents and teachers to meet to discuss the general class overview for the year. Children are not always invited to the back-to-school night. It is best to save specific questions regarding your child for a private conference, which you can arrange for a later time. (See section on parent-teacher conferences in the Parent Power chapter.)

How Teachers Are Contacted

Each school establishes procedures for parents who wish to contact teachers. Some schools provide voice mail or E-mail. Teachers should advise parents how they receive messages, their free hour in the day when they accept calls, and a reasonable time period within which you may expect a return call.

Homework Hotline

Is there a homework and/or school information hotline? This system allows parents and teachers to communicate quickly through any touch-tone telephone regarding classroom activities and homework assignments. By pressing access numbers, parents can hear a monthly calendar, up-to-date homework assignments, PTA activities, or other pertinent information. You may want to suggest this to your school if this service is not already available.

SCHOOL SUPPLIES AND MATERIALS

Restricted Items

It is important to learn the rules of the school for what is considered a restricted item. Radios, tape recorders, cameras, walkie-talkies, skateboards, video game cartridges, baseball cards, unauthorized sports equipment, pagers, cell phones and other items of value are not permitted at many schools.

Electronic Gadgets

This is the electronic era and gadgets abound. Some are useful learning devices, some are essential, and some are an unnecessary luxury. Laptop computers have increasing value and usefulness to students, even at the elementary school level. This technology eventually will serve as a supplement for students who have difficulty writing, who write slowly, or who have other graphomotor problems. Children never want to be different or look different, but if an electronic device such as a laptop computer or tape recorder assists learning, the child needs to be encouraged to use these accommodations. Suggest that your child try this accommodation as an experiment for one month. Agree to negotiate if it is too problematic when the month is up.

Other electronic learning devices are increasingly available. Electronic calendars and organizers make life easier, and many students have access to them. You might consider these for your child.

By middle school, supply needs may change. For example, scientific calculators may be required for math, and some classes require separate notebooks. Certain teachers may request the use of mechanical pencils or other special tools.

School Supplies to Keep at Home

Supplies that a child must provide will vary from school to school and from elementary to high school. For the elementary school child, keep a set of colored markers handy along with crayons, glue, safety scissors (left handed, if appropriate), number two pencils, lap board or desk, ruler, good lighting, yellow markers (to highlight their work), construction paper and an assignment book.

Teach your younger children how to use an assignment book from the very beginning; even a very simple one where they create their own assignment page is a good start. An older child may want to carry a small notebook for names and phone numbers of new friends and acquaintances.

As your child gets older, possession of or access to a computer with Internet and word processing capabilities is becoming more and more essential. In addition, we suggest having fact sheets available (commercially or self made) that list common spelling words, math facts, multiplication tables, geography facts and capitals. Other essential items include a dictionary (age appropriate), an atlas, a thesaurus, pencils and pens (either rollerball, ballpoint or felt tip, whichever your child prefers), three-by-five index cards, highlighters, a calculator, Liquid Paper, and paper.

Obtain a fresh notebook each semester and allow your child to participate in the choice. With a young child, set aside a special time for the two of you to set up and organize the notebooks. Remove materials that are no longer needed at school from the notebook, but keep them in a folder at home for future reference.

Encourage your child to choose a notebook with a clear plastic outside pocket so she can create her own cover design. One high school student created notebook cover inserts, using covers from her favorite CDs. These custom covers became icebreakers with other students and made it easier for her to meet people the first few days of school. Custom covers have added advantages in that they can be changed regularly with fresh and personalized content and they also help identify notebooks so they do not get lost. Replace worn-out notebooks quickly.

Be Prepared with School Supplies

Here is a list of suggested basic supplies most schools expect you to acquire for your child before starting each grade:

SCHOOL SUPPLIES

KINDERGARTEN
1 backpack or book bag
1 folder
1 box of crayons (8 basic colors) or markers
1 glue stick
1 towel or blanket for rest time

GRADE 1
1 backpack or book bag
1 school box of crayons, 24 colors
scissors
1 pink eraser
5 pencils sharpened
8 oz glue bottle
1 sharpened red pencil
2 folders
1 glue stick

GRADE 2
colored markers
2 folders
1 sharpened red pencil
1 pink eraser
5 pencils sharpened
1 backpack
supply box
8 oz glue bottle
1 glue stick

GRADE 3
Colored markers
1 pink eraser
6 pencils
wide-lined notebook paper
scissors
plastic pouch for pencils
1 plastic box for supplies
1 small set colored pencils
1 backpack
3 2-pocket folder
notebook
8 oz glue bottle
1 glue stick
ruler
fine tip markers
emergency money

GRADE 4
1" metal ring notebook
1 plastic box for supplies
markers or colored pencils
1 fine tip felt pen, red
scissors
1 12" ruler
1 standard compass
dividers, at least 4
plastic pouch
6 sharpened pencils
3x5 cards
1 yellow highlighter
1 8 oz glue bottle
glue stick

GRADES 5 AND 6
3 #2 pencils daily
2 blue/black pens
3-ring notebook paper
assignment book
2 red pencils
12 colored markers
3-ring divided notebook
P.E. clothes

GRADES 7 AND 8
1 ½" (3 ring) binder
dividers
notebook paper (wide ruled)
calculator (with name on it)
highlighter pen
5 pencils (sharpened)
2 red ink pens
2 spiral bound notebooks
1" binder for each class
stenographer pad
colored pencils for maps
pencil sharpener
2 erasable pens
ruler (metric & inched)

NOTES:

CONCLUSION

We hope these *SECRETS TO SCHOOL SUCCESS* will increase your knowledge and your optimism. Situations and unfolding life will provide ongoing opportunities to face dilemmas with creativity. We included our own experiences as psychologists and educators and we drew from the lives of our clients, families and friends. We are always learning new ideas and information from teachers and researchers. We trust you will benefit from this information and will incorporate it into your life and the lives of the people around you.

Our ideas are intended as beginnings. These are springboards that invite you to add your wisdom when resolving dilemmas. Individual circumstances and needs vary. We count on your creativity to adapt our suggestions to the uniqueness of your situations. We hope that many of our ideas and strategies will match your family's needs and will *guide your child through a joyous learning experience.*

Brandi Roth, Ph.D.
Fay Van Der Kar-Levinson, Ph.D.

ABOUT THE AUTHORS

Dr. Roth and Dr. Van Der Kar-Levinson are advisors to many therapeutic and educational organizations. They are popular seminar and media lecturers and the co-authors of *Choosing the Right School for Your Child.*

BRANDI ROTH, Ph.D.

Dr. Brandi Roth is a psychologist in private practice in Beverly Hills, California. She counsels children and adolescents with academic and behavioral problems. She specializes in conflict resolution with families, adults, adolescents and children. Dr. Roth's background as an educator includes public school teacher, educational therapist, program specialist, and advocate for special needs and gifted children.

FAY VAN DER KAR-LEVINSON, Ph.D.

Dr. Fay Van Der Kar-Levinson is a psychologist in private practice in West Los Angeles, California. She specializes in matching individual learning styles with appropriate educational programs. As a child development expert, Dr. Van Der Kar-Levinson provides consultation and support for parents and children.